Growing Your Small Business Made Simple

Wilbur Cross

Edited and prepared for publication by The Stonesong Press, Inc.

MADE SIMPLE BOOKS

A MADE SIMPLE BOOK

DOUBLEDAY

NEW YORK   LONDON   TORONTO   SYDNEY   AUCKLAND

Edited and prepared for publication by The Stonesong Press, Inc.

Executive Editor: Sheree Bykofsky

Series Editor: Sarah Gold

Copyeditor: Kathryn A. Clark

Production Consultant: *RECAP:* Publications, Inc.

Proofreader: Scarlett Smith

A MADE SIMPLE BOOK

Published by Doubleday, a division of
Bantam Doubleday Dell Publishing Group, Inc.
666 Fifth Avenue, New York, New York 10103

MADE SIMPLE and DOUBLEDAY are trademarks of Doubleday,
a division of Bantam Doubleday Dell Publishing Group, Inc.

Library of Congress Cataloging-in-Publication Data
Cross, Wilbur.
     Growing your small business made simple/Wilbur Cross. — 1st ed.
       p.   cm.
     "A Made Simple book."
     Includes index.
     1. Small business — Management.   I. Title.
HD62.7.C76   1993
658.02'2 — dc20   92-21350
ISBN 0-385-42429-9   CIP

CONTENTS

PART THREE: MARKETING

Ready for Growth

Many readers of this book may find the title familiar, having already read the previous business volume in the Doubleday series, *Your Small Business Made Simple*, by Richard Gallagher. Even if you own or manage a business that is already established, you may benefit from reading that work. It contains many fundamentals that are well worth reviewing.

This companion volume, *Growing Your Small Business Made Simple*, is the ideal follow-up. It reexamines many of the subjects covered in the earlier volume, exploring them in terms of the small business that is growing, extending its capabilities, and perhaps diversifying into new fields. You may be in retailing and want to add a new product line. Or you may have created a service that has been popular and now you see a way to add a complementary service that is needed. Or perhaps you have an opportunity to expand your facilities and increase your production. This book will give you some practical pointers on managing these various opportunities for growth.

The text also delves into those special problems and challenges that are posed when a small business grows, and gives instruction on how to direct that growth in a steady and properly planned, rather than explosive, manner. Chapter by chapter, this book holds out the promise that small businesses can be made to grow and prosper in good health when the right plans are formulated and the right procedures employed. You will find realistic assessments of the pitfalls that accompany overexpansion, too-rapid expansion, and risky diversification into incompatible fields.

How do you know when your business is ready to grow? The growth stage of an organization is characterized by more accelerated progress, the consolidation and strengthening of the venture's status, an ascending achievement curve, a growing number of employees, an increase in managers and supervisors, improved capitalization, and strong evidence of physical and material acquisitions.

If you can steer your business carefully through the growth stage, eventually it will achieve maturity, the point at which the typical small business can be expected to reach its ultimate capabilities. This volume will guide you in methods and plans for avoiding the stagnation that can set in at this stage and thus allow your business to remain economically healthy and continue to grow.

PART ONE

EVALUATING GROWTH AND PLANNING ITS MANAGEMENT

CHAPTER ONE

Charting the Business Life Cycle

KEY TERMS FOR THIS CHAPTER

acquisitions	*entrepreneur*	*initial stage*
business life cycle	*explosive growth*	*internal growth*
controlled growth	*external growth*	*maturity*
decline	*growth and expansion stage*	*mergers, horizontal*
diversification	*holding operation*	*mergers, vertical*

When you started your business, you saw growth as a desirable objective. You may have contemplated one or more types of growth, such as enlarging your physical plant and other facilities, increasing the ranks of managers and employees, acquiring subsidiaries, escalating sales, or diversifying into new products and/or services. Many small businesses have grown in several or all of these ways and eventually rounded the corner into the realm of big business.

The fact that your venture has grown measurably shows that you picked the right business at the right time and that you combined the necessary basics to get it well launched and keep it headed upward. Now it is time to step back, be as objective as possible, and take a considered overview of the **business life cycle**. This cycle will provide a clue to the future success or failure of your business.

The Four Stages of the Business Life Cycle

Businesses, like human beings, are born, begin to grow, are healthy or become sick, mature, and inevitably decline and die. A large number attain only one or two stages before passing out of the picture, and a few manage to pass through the full cycle before they, too, disappear.

The concept of the business life cycle is succinctly summed up in a course prospectus distributed to graduate students at the Fuqua

ZERO GROWTH

After months of research, Loretta Collins decided that the small town she had moved to in central New Hampshire needed a bookstore. She had come from a Boston suburb, where she and her friends and neighbors were accustomed to stopping by the local bookstore two or three times a month. She carefully checked all the factors and, with the help of her accountant, decided that, once it was established, a bookstore in her new location would provide her with a tidy annual income as well as a satisfying pursuit.

The nearest bookstore of any consequence was at the county seat, 25 miles away over a winding road. The residents of her town included many retirees, as well as urbanites who owned vacation homes there; most of them regular readers of books and were interested in cultural matters. And there were at least a dozen local authors in the vicinity who might stimulate business with in-store autograph receptions. Moreover, she could lease an attractive store in the center of town for a modest sum, since it had been vacant for two years and the owners were willing to accept a low rent for a one-year period.

Six months after opening The Bookshelf, Ms. Collins felt that she was well on her way. She had established some regular customers and had found inexpensive ways to advertise and promote the new store. There were no profits in sight, but she had not expected a breakthrough before the end of the first year. Then, she faced a series of disheartening setbacks.

The first was one she should have anticipated: the completion of a new wing at the local library with the addition of a Popular Reading Room, where library users could browse and borrow best-sellers and other current works. This all but killed the Bookshelf's own Lending Den, where daily loan rates were four times that of the public library, and seriously cut back the purchase of new releases.

The second big reversal was the addition of a paperback book section in the town's main supermarket, which offered a large range of titles at discount.

By the end of the year, Loretta admitted defeat and informed her landlord she would not be renewing the store lease. She managed to avoid bankruptcy by returning much of her stock to publishers and selling the rest wholesale to the supermarket and the town library.

School of Business of Duke University in Durham, North Carolina, which concludes, "The manager who not only understands, but accepts, this historic life cycle will hold a distinct advantage over the renegade who is determined to outsmart history."

For the purpose of evaluating your own venture, think in terms of these four stages:

1. The **initial stage,** during which you perfect the concepts of your enterprise, formally establish the business in the location and manner intended, and communicate your intentions to the extent needed to get under way.

2. The **growth and expansion stage,** characterized by progress that can be measured in terms of professional achievements and finan-

cial assets and an increase in productive activity and the number of people involved.

3. Maturity, which is the plateau reached when the organization's growth and expansion have leveled off and cannot realistically be expected to increase.

4. Decline, the final stage, which may occur abruptly or over a long period of time, during which the organization as it was originally conceived can only be expected to go down.

Let's take a look at these stages in detail and review some examples of small businesses that are found in each stage.

The Initial Stage

A business is born when an **entrepreneur** is struck by an idea that can be parlayed into a going concern, make profits, and grow. What criteria determine whether the idea can take root and achieve these goals?

• There is a consumer or community need for the product(s) or service(s) involved

• The founder has the experience and knowledge to pursue the idea

• Enough capital is available, or can be acquired, to launch the venture and maintain its momentum

• A suitable location is available

• The population can support this kind of business

• The local economy is healthy enough to provide potential income

• Suitable employees and, if necessary, qualified specialists can be easily recruited

• The business is not likely to be overly sensitive to economic fluctuations, changing consumer tastes, or political legislation

• There are no legal entanglements or judiciary risks that could result in setbacks or heavy expenses

• Competition is light or non-existent.

The entrepreneur launches a venture with the expectation that it will take time — perhaps a year or so — for the business to take hold and reach a break-even point. This introductory period is the most precarious stage and the one in which most failures occur.

Even though you may be steadily adding employees, some with limited authority, the initial stage is one in which you hold a tight rein on the business, controlling all the major management and operational functions. This is necessary in order to make sure the venture is taking hold. This state of the business has been referred to by some experts as a **holding operation,** in that certain decisions must be held in abeyance while you wait for favorable signs to proceed, or negative signs to abort the venture before you lose your shirt.

The initial stage can be expected to continue for a year or two, longer in the case of a more complicated enterprise. In naval terminology, this would be called a "shakedown cruise," its duration and complexity depending upon the size of the ship.

The Period of Growth and Expansion

Following the initial stage, the business moves into the phase the entrepreneur has been waiting for: accelerating progress, growth, and finally, profits. Among the first clues that this stage is being reached are:

• Recognition in the industry
• An ascending sales curve
• Repeat customers, patrons, or clients
• Improved financial status in the eyes of local banks and investment specialists
• A growing number of employees
• The addition of managers and supervisors and the evolution of several layers of management

AN IDEAL GROWTH STAGE

Unlike unfortunate Loretta Collins, Ira and Doreen Postner found their bookish pursuit to be a real joy and a substantial income producer. They, too, had moved to a small town, in this case in North Carolina, in a region known for the manufacture of furniture. Avid readers themselves, they became aware that it was difficult to purchase current books without driving more than 30 miles to the nearest city, and even then they found that what they wanted was often out of stock or not yet on the shelves.

After conducting research, they decided that their new community could support a small bookstore. There were many devoted readers like themselves in the community; there was excellent space for lease at a new mall; and they could get adequate financing from one of the local banks.

The Postners opened their emporium. But it was quite different from what they had originally conceived. It was a *juvenile* bookstore, which they named Magic Moments in Print. The concept was original enough to garner publicity in local newspapers and broadcasts and, of course, a considerable amount of backing from schools and parental organizations, whose members were interested in encouraging young people to read. As time went on, the booksellers kept themselves in the public eye (and ear) by promoting books as prizes for achievements by young people in all fields of activity, from academics to sports.

What convinced the Postners to specialize in this manner was a report from the American Booksellers Association (ABA) that sales of children's books were almost 20 percent higher than those of adult fiction and non-fiction. They also learned, through research by the American Library Association (ALA), that children's books in small-town libraries across America were being borrowed far more than those on the adult shelves.

The Postners promoted new books and reading pleasures through their "Magic Moments" theme and related activities. "We created a contest in which young people described their 'Most Magic Moment' while reading a book," said Doreen Postner. "This stimulated a great deal of interest in our store and helped to sell a lot of books."

MMP, as the store has become known, has diversified in a minor way, adding a line of greeting cards specially designed for young people and a Nature Corner, which displays and sells such items as bird houses, hamster cages, miniature flower gardens, small acquariums, ant farms, and seashell collections.

The Postners' small business reached the break-even point after ten months of operation and was well into the black before the end of the first year. During the past two years, the founders have conducted research and are convinced the business will grow for at least a decade, then level off for a few years before going into any kind of decline. They figure, however, that they will probably sell the business before their tenth anniversary and retire on the profits.

- The need for increased capitalization
- The need for, and purchase of, new capital equipment
- A need for relocation and/or spatial additions.

The Maturity Stage

As the growth stage starts to level off, one of two things will happen to the conventional small business: it will show signs of plunging, leading the owner to sell the business (if possible) or make plans to phase it out and liquidate it in an orderly manner; or it will continue on a generally level course into a state of maturity.

According to C. Allen Scharf, an expert on mergers, acquisitions, and takeovers, maturity is a phase that often discourages entrepreneurs. Managers who formerly were very aggressive become docile and lazy. Some start looking around for other business enterprises to join. And, as he commented, "The only people who benefit are the wives of formerly workaholic executives who now seem to be coming home from the office on time — or earlier — and who seldom have to work anymore on Saturdays and holidays."

A SERENE MATURITY

Walking into the cool, dark recesses of the Old Emporium in Chesterville, Vermont, one has the distinct impression of being in the late 1800s, when it was founded as the village general store. The atmosphere is much the same, though the items on the counters and shelves are somewhat fancier than the harness grease, cornmeal, and pitchforks that were commonplace at the turn of the century.

When Steve and Marla Pockett decided to reactivate the old family business, they took a dream and transformed it into reality. The building had been boarded up for years, but within eleven months they had meticulously restored the exterior and interior with the help of old photographs. And they had proved they could intrigue a new generation with homemade marinades and dressings, fancy mustards, Victorian dessert toppings, and fine herb breads concocted from century-old recipes. These were sold not just in the store, which was frequented by vacationers as well as townsfolk, but through prime retail outlets across the country. One of their toughest problems was obtaining and processing enough local ingredients to supply prestigious big-city specialty stores with products to meet the demand.

The Old Emporium has become a tourist attraction and will remain one for at least a generation to come. But the product sales have leveled off and the venture has reached a venerable stage of maturity which should continue for as long as the Pocketts care to stay in business. To try to move up from this plateau to a new pattern of growth would require an investment almost equal to the annual profits.

"So we continue to ride along and enjoy the locale and the business and our many friends, old and new," says Marla. "We've accomplished what we set out to do."

ENDING WITH A BANG

Philip Holland is the successful founder and president of the largest privately owned doughnut-shop chain in the United States. But he was not always so successful.

At the age of 34, Holland founded a contracting business based on a premise of "total responsibility." He attracted clients by assuring them that his firm would carry out all aspects of development, including architecture and design, site selection and preparation, financing, construction, and property management on a contract basis. Over a period of ten years, his company prospered, building at least 150 projects, mainly small apartment buildings on the West Coast.

"By the end of the second year," he explained, "I had earned a reputation as the chap who in thought, word, and deed was a business genius and always a sure winner. Success went to my head. I became blind to the idea of failure and simply overlooked some of the clues that would have been obvious to a more discerning businessman."

Among the clues that Holland disregarded were these:

- A surplus of apartments was being built in the areas in which he operated, as was readily apparent from the increasing number of vacancies listed in the real-estate section of local papers.
- Financing for apartments and other residences was drying up.
- Experienced employees were being lured away from the construction field into other fields which offered higher salaries and more benefits.
- His unwieldy carrying costs were not being offset by comparable sales, because he was overproducing the market.

The outcome soon became obvious. Within a few months the Holland enterprise reached the end of its growth stage, the beginning of maturity, and the decline stage. The company went bankrupt. It eventually paid off its debts, largely because the next venture was very successful and Holland made every possible effort to regain his reputation in the community.

But a few entrepreneurs really relish the time when their brainchildren reach maturity because it frees them to plan other ventures. Seldom, however, do they make the mistake of letting the old business go to pot. They guard their assets and resources tenaciously. In some cases they even stimulate new periods of temporary growth — perhaps because of upsurges in the economy, a sudden need for their products or services, or changes in the character of the local population. This stage is also known as "activated maturity."

Eventually, every small business, no matter how successful, will reach its limits in terms of performance, need, size, and income. There are no charts or business barometers to determine in advance when this period of maturity will begin, how long it will last, or when it will end in a pronounced decline. Many a small business has grown into a large entity by the time it has matured. The reverse is equally true, as is the case when a corporation retains its economic core but keeps phasing out or selling off various divisions and affiliates.

When growth becomes difficult to measure, a company can be classed as mature.

The Decline Stage

A no-growth situation can continue for decades, but signs of decline will become evident very quickly: End-of-the-year profits are harder to come by; employees start drifting away and recruiting new employees becomes a chore; the costs of upkeep for offices and facilities climb relentlessly; the atmosphere becomes more subdued; and middle managers and supervisors stop working overtime.

This period of decline is naturally dreaded by the owners of small businesses. The length of time required for the final stage in the business life cycle is often a matter of management foresight, evaluation, and decision-making about a sensible method for concluding the business. The alternatives are to sell while the business still has some financial value; to declare bankruptcy, if the downhill trend has been more abrupt and disruptive than expected; or to shut the doors formally, having alerted all employees, suppliers, the media, and everyone else concerned.

How to Plan Growth

Controlled vs. Explosive Growth

Explosive growth — when a business suddenly takes off and runs — should be viewed with

skepticism rather than with jubilation. "Unprecedented initial success," warned one new-business consultant, "often leads to serious complications."

James Silvester, a professor of small business management and director of the Small Business Institute at Shenandoah College in Virginia, has this to say about managing growth:

"Growing too fast can be as hazardous as a no-growth situation, if not more so. Growth must be implemented and managed carefully to insure that the business does not expand beyond its ability to control and/or finance operation. Many firms have met with demise because of uncontrollable expansion." He adds that growth, in order to be managed effectively, must be mapped out well in advance, evaluating the company's resources necessary to handle estimated expansion. "If resources will be lacking because of internal constraints and/or environmental factors," he cautions, "expansion objectives should be altered to meet with the realities of the situation."

Mark McCormack, a highly successful entrepreneur and author of the best-selling book *What They Don't Teach You at the Harvard Business School,* says of the first six years spent in his small business venture, "I also wanted to get better before we got bigger. So many companies, particularly in this high-tech age, are unwilling to do this. They would rather grow quickly than profit quickly. If these companies would slow down a little, take some time to analyze their success, and allow their depth of management to catch up, I think they would see that they could have both — a healthy growth rate and healthy profitability."

McCormack points out that he realized early on that his own small business could not stay the same size. But he resisted, and continued to resist, the pressure to grow too fast. "A lot of business," he says, "is listening to your own common sense, then taking the necessary steps to turn the theories into practice."

Controlled growth is vital in the case of small businesses, which simply cannot afford to make the kind of trial-and-error mistakes that a large corporation can readily absorb. You need a realistic growth plan, which should incorporate the following elements:

- Major objectives, such as sales levels, physical plants, or number of potential customers or clients
- Schedules for consolidating the stages and attaining goals
- Additions of managers and supervisors
- Labor recruitment plans and employee charts and specifications
- Procedures for locating and tapping necessary resources, such as materials, goods, and supplies
- Meeting financial needs, overall and for specific projects and developments

- The assignment of qualified coordinators to expedite the total growth plan.

All of these areas will be considered in detail in later chapters.

Internal vs. External Growth

If you maintain a family-owned business, sell stock to friends and relatives, acquire partners on a personal level, and plow profits back into the venture, you can generate appreciable **internal growth.** This growth can be further enhanced by adding new products, creating new services, or acquiring more capital. Internal growth is generally slower than external growth but has the advantage of remaining under more stringent control.

External growth is accomplished through a number of means. The most common are:

- Going public and issuing common stock

RUNAWAY GROWTH PATTERNS

Certain factors can be clues to runaway growth, signaling future disaster in an otherwise healthy business climate. The following symptoms, among others, indicate that growth is out of control:

- Excessive costs of doing business
- Breakdowns in internal communication
- Problems in coordination among departments
- Confusion about management responsibilities
- Dissatisfied employees
- Increasing personnel turnover
- Too many employees with time on their hands
- Explosive paperwork demands

EXTERNAL FACTORS AFFECTING GROWTH

The Small Business Administration suggests that owners of growing small businesses keep their eye on ten key demographic and business factors that may affect the growth of their venture:

1. The state of the industry or field in which the business functions
2. Reliable government and private forecasts for the future of the industry
3. The condition of the national economy
4. The condition of the local economy
5. The nature and status of immediate competition
6. Growth or decline in the ranks of prospective customers, patrons, and clients
7. The availability of prospective employees who are reliable and experienced in pertinent areas of expansion
8. Scientific, technological, or other specialized developments that might affect future business
9. Political conditions and events that could impact on future growth
10. Your own expectations and plans in regard to the future of the business and your continuous participation in it.

- Becoming a franchisee
- Acquiring another organization in a similar or related field
- Merging with another company.

External growth is generally faster than internal growth. In the case of going public, for example, you acquire capital more quickly than through the internal expansion of business. As for franchising, you receive support and usually supplies or equipment through the franchisor — things that would take longer to acquire through strictly internal growth.

In the case of **mergers** and **acquisitions,** you obtain measurable strengths right away, such as employees, facilities, and other physical assets.

Mergers and acquisitions fall into two categories:

1. Horizontal, in which similar business operations are combined to increase the whole (such as two hotels, chains of retail boutiques, or service stations).

2. Vertical, in which the participants are up or down the operational mode from each other (such as a wholesale outlet combining with a manufacturer of the goods sold, or a warehouse joining with a trucking firm supplying the transportation of goods stored).

Growth Through Diversification

Once your small business is established and running well, you may get the itch to try **diversification** into other fields. Generally, small businesses diversify into areas that bear some relationship to the original venture, but more adventuresome entrepreneurs may try their hands at something entirely new. Diversification into new businesses, whether related or unrelated, represents one of the highest risks you can take. According to the National Business Information Center, fewer than 20 percent of the small businesses in America have been successful when they tried to diversify. And that list includes only those businesses that were recognized as being successful prior to diversification.

The chief reasons for failure are:

- Poor selection of enterprises into which to diversify
- Lack of experience in, or knowledge about, the new areas of business
- Allocating too much investment capital to an untried field
- Overloading managers with additional commitments
- Neglecting existing business in order to attend to the new one.

The best way to maximize your chance of success is to be alert to the problems as well as the potential.

Who Will Succeed You?

No matter which course of action you select, don't ignore one vital issue: the matter of succession. Many small-business owners see themselves as indefatigable and indispensable. The late Arthur Gompert, who trained two generations of small-business managers, used to advise entrepreneurs to "take four weeks off and make yourself totally unavailable. If you return and find your company in a sad state of disrepair, then you don't have a going business at all."

Be sure, as your business grows, that there are managers who can make decisions in your absence and that you are training your successor to carry the business forward.

Risk-taking

By the time your enterprise has reached the growth stage, it is well enough along to allow you to take calculated risks that will help it to grow. This growth may be vertical, that is, remaining in the same field but doing business in greater depth. For instance, an art gallery selling original paintings might add sculptures as well. Or the growth could be horizontal, becoming involved with other related fields of business. In the case of the art gallery, the owner could decide to add a line of artist's supplies to the business. In certain cases, the growth could be a combination of both, yet still retain the initial image of the enterprise.

The risk element lies in the fact that you sometimes have to make decisions to take a course of action without having conclusive evidence that you are doing the right thing. While you cannot avoid all the uncertainties and gambles, your level of risk is less when you make forceful commitments at a time when you are firmly established and can be reasonably sure of the outcome. The following rules will help you reduce the risks, while at the same time giving you enough leeway to shoot for higher objectives:

Rule Number One: Never get involved in a venture that is speculative and at the same time calls for you to put most of your assets at stake.

Rule Number Two: If you are good at your basic business, stick with it and related enterprises rather than plunging into the unknown.

Rule Number Three: Test the waters before you plunge in. It is well worth the investment of money and time to investigate the nature of a risk venture.

Rule Number Four: Determine realistically how much of a drain on your present business the risk venture will be before you are able to stabilize it.

STATISTICS FOR THE BUSINESS CYCLE

According to Dun & Bradstreet, the survival odds for a small business are about 50/50 during the first five years. After that, some 75 percent of the businesses that are still functioning will manage to grow or at least hold their own for another five years. After that, about three out of every four enterprises that have celebrated their first decade will continue through the second decade and even beyond.

The following table illustrates the failure rate for an average year:

Age of Venture	All Kinds General*	Manufac- turing	Wholesale Trade	Retail Trade	Services
1 year	10.0%	7.8%	7.7%	12.0%	14.9%
2 years	12.4	13.0	12.5	15.9	12.7
3 years	11.4	11.3	11.3	13.7	11.2
4 years	9.4	9.9	9.5	10.1	8.9
5 years	7.5	7.0	8.4	7.6	7.8
Total, five years or less:	50.7%	49.0%	49.4%	59.3%	55.5%
Six to ten years:	24.6%	23.3%	25.5%	22.0%	24.6%
Over ten years:	24.7%	27.7%	25.1%	18.7%	19.9%

* "General" includes the four listed in the columns, plus construction, mining, forestry, agriculture, fishing, transportation, insurance, real estate, finance, recreation, sports, health, and utilities.

"Twin" Cases: Success and Failure in the Growth Stage

Below are brief accounts of three pairs of firms. The members of a pair are in the same type of business and reach the same market. They are "twins," with a critical exception: One is a glorious success, the other a dismal failure. (Company names and some details have been changed to protect the identities of the entrepreneurs.)

Side-stepping to Success

• Ralph Gorman was reasonably successful in his printing business, mainly filling orders for local business firms. But he found that his business tended to be seasonal, forcing him to work long hours for weeks on end, then leaving him with little to do for a like amount of time. His wife kept wondering why the business couldn't be extended to help small customers (like herself) who wanted something printed, but whose jobs were too small for conventional printers. The Gormans formed PEP (Personal Expert Printers), geared to overnight printing of small jobs for non-business customers. Their business grew quickly and has been on the upswing for more than five years.

• Sensing the need for quick, economical printing, the father and son owners of Belleau & Son stationery supplies added a side office and began soliciting orders for print jobs under the name Day-At-A-Time Producers. They then made arrangements with several commercial printers to do the work and obtained samples of designs and typography to display in their sales office. They already had plenty of paper samples because of their stationery services and were convinced the extension of the business would be a cinch. Within a matter of months, they were at odds with all of their suppliers and were constantly apologizing to customers for delays and errors.

Why did the Gormans succeed while the Belleaus failed?

The former saw their business grow swiftly because they owned the basic printing facilities and thus were able to exert managerial control over the production jobs promised to customers. The latter failed because they had to rely on outsiders who continually postponed the Gormans' small orders when they had large, more profitable, printing contracts. This fact, as well as deadline pressures, led to typos and other printing errors and a poor business image.

Baby Boom Bonanza

• Janet Gaylord and her sister, Jenny, had an idea. Why not capitalize on the fact that most new parents are eager to share their joy with the world and to proclaim to everyone about the recent addition to the family. The result of their creative thinking was Borrow-A-Stork, which offered a single item for rent: a plastic stork in a baby bonnet, with a simulated bundle of joy dangling from its beak for proud new parents to display in the yard or at the front door. The bird, standing six feet tall, cost about $50 to produce and was easily rentable for $40 a week. As their reputation grew, the sisters added other rentables, such as giant cardboard birthday cakes, life-size plywood clowns, and banners proclaiming "It's a Boy (or Girl)." Their business grew as they steadily extended their market area and added new "event rentables" to the line.

• A producer of displays for department stores and other retailers had developed a steady business, but could not seem to expand it. So, with the help of a partner who had an imaginative turn of mind, he created a line of consumer display items to be produced in their commercial plant but sold in a shop they leased, under the name Happy Happenings. These items were symbols of events, much like the stork, birthday cake, and birth announcements created by the Borrow-A-Stork partners. The difference was that they were to be sold to customers, not rented. The business started off with a bang, achieving a great deal of publicity in the local press. But then it slumped and was eventually discontinued.

Why did the Gaylord sisters succeed and the commercial display partners fail?

The Gaylords had the management sense to learn two truths in advance: first, people would pay up to a certain amount to do something dramatic to help celebrate an event. Second, they not only wanted to limit the budget, but they didn't want to have to store ungainly items that were too expensive to throw away. The owners of Happy Happenings lost out because they failed to incorporate the consumers' short-term interest in their marketing plan and thus tried to sell, rather than rent, their products.

Beat the Heat and Reap the Profit

• Tired of fighting snow and ice, Sarah and Sam Halbrook moved to the South. They soon found that one of the drawbacks of living in a semi-tropical clime was that every time they returned to their car, the front seat was searing hot from the sun streaming through the windshield. Sarah came up with the solution: a cardboard cut-out that could be placed inside the windshield to block the glare. It worked so well that she made a few for friends and decorated them with flowers and animals. Before she knew it, she and Sam had a small cottage industry, which they labelled S&S, for their initials and the words Sun & Shade.

The Halbrooks used the windshield screen as their base product and then created other "sun and shade" products for the home, the office, the patio, and the beach. They also increased the market by devising a sideline of windshield screens with printed and pictorial adds, which they marketed to local businesses for giveaways and customer incentives. Their venture has flourished.

• In Southern California another husband and wife team, Howie and Alda Reneer, came up with the same idea. Their initial business success was almost the same. But then it leveled off, limping along for a couple of years before the imaginative entrepreneurs scrapped their business.

Why did the Halbrooks' business grow steadily while their West Coast peers, the Reneers, were unable to move much beyond the break-even point?

The answer lies in the ability to manage for growth. The California entrepreneurs obviously had a sound, marketable idea. But their market was a stable one, composed largely of residents. Unlike the Florida market, it did not include a steady influx of *new* prospects — tourists, vacationers, and visiting relatives, who might find the products attractive. In retrospect, they realized that, once they had saturated the existing market, there were few new prospects for sales. And they had nothing else to offer the original customers in order to generate repeat business.

The Halbrooks, on the other hand, reviewed the sales pattern early on and foresaw what would happen, moving into sidelines to keep their business growing.

CHAPTER TWO

Making a Profile of Your Business

KEY TERMS FOR THIS CHAPTER

capitalizing	*policies*
consultant	*procedures*
corporation	*profile*
financing	*sole proprietorship*
partnership	

Before you can evaluate your small business's growth possibilities, you need to prepare a **profile** of the enterprise. This profile should describe clearly the nature of the business, the type of product or service you offer, and the advantages your business has over the competition — particularly nearby competitors. The plan must explore the opportunities for immediate success and the potential for growth, preferably over a period of at least five years.

Preparing the Profile

Think of the profile as a kind of corporate resume. The people you are trying most to impress are likely to be outsiders, such as potential investors, lawyers, or consultants. Among other things, you may want them to

- Join the venture
- Invest in it
- Give approval for legal and government specifications
- Authorize financial involvement or support by their organization
- Publicize your plans or key personnel
- Provide professional advice.

Elements of a Business Profile

A good business plan must accomplish the following objectives:

- Identify you and your business partners (if you have any) with details about your qualifications, experience, and dedication to the effort.
- Identify where the business is headquartered and the geographical areas in which it functions or into which you want it to expand.
- Evaluate the customers, clients, or others whose monetary contributions will determine the success or failure of the expansion.
- Offer realistic assessment of direct and marginal competitors.
- Detail an acceptable method for **capitalizing** and **financing** the proposed expansion.
- Outline a timetable estimating when future expansion is expected to occur, what specific functions will be involved, and how long it will take for any new ventures to reach the break-even point.

A business plan, while not infallible, can reveal how thoroughly you have developed your concepts of growth. The very act of projecting these vital elements will not only indicate the chances of success or failure, but it will also serve as a guideline for reorganizing the company and introducing it to potential employees and clients.

Composing the Plan

If you are not experienced at developing and submitting proposals and presentations, it is advisable to hire a **consultant**. This step should be taken after you have prepared a rough draft of the proposal and outlined the elements that you think should be incorporated into the finished presentation. An experienced consultant will then be able to ask intelligent questions, work with you quickly and effectively, and at a lower cost than if he or she needed to start from scratch.

A good, solid plan is based on the assumption that you are going to continue to succeed. Yet, that is not, in itself, sufficient. Success can mean any number of things, or a combination of things, such as:

- Monetary profit
- Offering a much-needed service to your community
- Providing more jobs for the region
- Losing money, but serving to reduce taxes for a parent organization
- Providing an environment for a company's growth.

You must decide what success means for your business, and focus your profile to make it clear how you can achieve that success.

Your approach should be positive and optimistic. Yet it must also be forthright and address the challenges that have to be considered.

When the text has been drafted and revised, take time to make a test presentation to friends or colleagues who are not involved with your business and who can give you an objective opinion. This will not only help you to detect weaknesses in the proposal but will give you the confidence to present it to strangers.

The chances are that your business profile will be directed at an audience of professionals: bankers, attorneys, investors, specialists, technologists, managers, executives, and accountants, to name a few. These professionals expect to read facts and figures, not wishful thinking. They have read many proposals and listened to many presentations by entrepreneurs eager to expand their small businesses, and they can quickly spot flaws and omissions in a plan.

In writing any business operational plan or profile, think of the people you are trying to reach as pros. That does not mean that you

AN OUTLINE FOR YOUR BUSINESS GROWTH PROFILE

1. An Overview
   - Proposed renaming of the company
   - Changing nature of venture
   - Revisions of specific objectives
2. Physical Description
   - Real estate required for growth
   - Necessary facilities needed for expansion
   - New equipment and supplies required
   - Location changes or additions
   - Increase in transportation, owned or leased
3. Economics
   - Annual dollar volume, with projections
   - Further capitalization needed
   - Projected sales (or similar) figures
   - Loan requirements, if any
   - Changes in insurance premiums
   - Additional taxes expected
4. Personnel
   - Increase in managers, number and type
   - Increase in employees, number and skills
   - Part-time employees and/or consultants required
   - Training required, initial and ongoing
5. Marketing and Advertising
   - Changes in customer/client demographics
   - Additional competitors, known or anticipated
   - New marketing functions to be established
   - Projected advertising budget and media
   - Sales promotion tools to be needed
   - Public relations functions, present and future
   - Variations in product pricing and/or service charges
   - Changing needs for suppliers and servicers
   - Projected inventory control

have to use fancy language or ingenious devices to gain their attention. It does mean that you should be direct, honest, and positive.

Areas to Review: Structure, Commitments, Goals, and Policies

The Legal Structure of Your Business

You should now reevaluate the legal structure you initially selected for your business and decide whether it is the most propitious for future growth, or whether you should change. Your three fundamental choices are:

1. A **sole proprietorship,** in which you are the owner of the business and call the signals.
2. A **partnership,** in which two or more people manage the business, make decisions, and are jointly responsible and liable for the actions that take place.
3. A **corporation,** which is structured so that officers can be changed according to the consent of the directors and in which managers have only limited liability in the event of failure or legal action.

As your business grows, you may find it advantageous to revise the organizational structure from a sole proprietorship to a partnership or corporation — or the reverse. A great deal depends upon the human element: how well people at all levels work together and accomplish the stated objectives. For the tax implications of these various structures, see Chapter Five.

Commitments

Any evaluation of the structure of an organization and its later growth has to review very carefully the initial commitments that were made to people who are in any way involved with, or affected by, the business. These include: customers or clients, investors, suppliers, associated organizations, residents of the community, government officials, employees, and families of employees, among others. As you prepare your profile, ask yourself these questions:

- Which commitments were honored?
- Which were neglected?
- Which have remained in limbo?
- Which were unrealistic?

For example, originally you might have set certain deadlines for supplying products or services and then realized that you were too optimistic. Or salary increases might have been slower to take effect than originally projected. Or you could have promised rights and permissions that have now turned out to be contestable.

Project future commitments in terms of past and current growth and communicate this updated version of your intentions to all individuals and groups that are concerned.

Goals and Objectives

Review the goals and objectives you specified in the original proposal for your small business, or which you stated to potential investors, partners, associates, suppliers, bankers, clients, or others who were essential to the success of the enterprise. Perhaps profit was your primary goal for the business when it started and now you feel that expansion into new markets should take priority. Or you may have hoped to be in a location where you could obtain labor at a lower pay scale, but now you see that it is more important to pay higher salaries and upgrade the skills of the available labor pool. Or you may have envisioned the business as one that would remain private but have since come to believe that it would grow more substantially if it went public.

Ask yourself these questions:

- Which goals and objectives are still vital?
- Which have proved to be unrealistic?
- What additional goals should be considered to implement further growth?
- How might my business's objectives change in the near future?

WORKSHEET FOR A BUSINESS PROFILE

Check the answer alongside each element of the business to determine where most of the growth has occurred. If the worksheet shows that certain areas have had strong or moderate growth, then you should be revising your operational plans for these functions. If more than one-third reflect such growth changes (or losses), then you may well need to reorganize your entire company.

In some cases, the reorganization of a particular sector may be relatively simple, as in the matter of hiring additional employees. In other cases, though, such changes can be complex and comprehensive — as you might expect, for example, in adjusting your administration and management. Your first step is to chart the growth patterns:

Key Business Areas	Strong Growth	Moderate Growth	No Growth	Loss
Administration and management	___	___	___	___
Gross income	___	___	___	___
Net income	___	___	___	___
Personnel in management	___	___	___	___
Number of supervisors	___	___	___	___
Total employees	___	___	___	___
Real estate	___	___	___	___
Holdings	___	___	___	___
Markets	___	___	___	___
Share of market (or similar)	___	___	___	___
Image in community	___	___	___	___
Image in industry	___	___	___	___
Equity, in toto	___	___	___	___
Customers or clients	___	___	___	___
Suppliers	___	___	___	___
Advertising and promotion	___	___	___	___
Production capabilities	___	___	___	___
Training and orientation	___	___	___	___

It is a good idea to list all of these goal — both old and new — on paper, for internal discussion and revision. Once listed, they should be arranged in order of priority and then in chronological sequence, if that is significant.

You should not end up with a long "laundry list," but rather with a tightly knit grouping of essential goals and objectives. If you have too many, you will never achieve all of them, and it will be difficult to set priorities.

Once you have determined your basic goals for continuing growth, communicate them to the people who count, both within your business and outside it. These could be your managers and employees, customers and clients, investors, and residents of the community.

The Formation of Policies and Procedures

Business **policies** and **procedures,** said a successful entrepreneur, are often like moths. They flare up as they fly into a bright light, then fade away and disappear as they vanish into the darkness. Express your policies and procedures *in writing*. If you cannot explain them on paper, then they need to be rethought or even scrapped.

Policies, of course, change as the business changes or as external circumstances may dictate. Some companies that have long had dress-code policies, for example, have recently been the target of successful lawsuits by employees claiming such dictates infringed on their rights.

Whenever you formulate a business policy, ask yourself these questions:

- Is the policy essential to the business?
- Is it stable and durable?
- Is it legal, or at least within the spirit of the law?
- How should it be communicated internally?
- Does the policy need to be communicated externally?
- Does it jibe with the direction in which you want your company to grow?
- Does it face up to setbacks and problems in a realistic manner?
- Is it in keeping with the current status of the company?

CHAPTER THREE

Appraising the Business Climate

KEY TERMS FOR THIS CHAPTER

climate of risk
competitive climate
demographic climate
downtrends
economic climate

economic indicators
erosion of profits
recession-proof
risk management

No small business can be an island unto itself and expect to prosper for long. Not only must you take a serious look at the various aspects of your business, as we saw in chapter two, but you would also be wise to conduct regular analyses of the business world around you. Three main factors for you to assess are the economy, competition, and demographics. These factors are known as "climates;" that is, they constitute the environmental conditions in which your business operates. Understanding how each of these factors affects your business will help you to keep it growing on course.

Economic Climate

One of these external factors, and a key one, is the factor we refer to as the **economic climate.** This is simply a phrase that describes the state of the economy nationally, regionally, and locally. Is the country in a recession? On an upswing? Normal? The local climate can be different from the national one, however — as in the case where real estate sales are generally down nationwide, but steady, or even improving, in certain locales.

No matter how fast your business has grown, or how sound your management or product or services may be, if the economic climate is unhealthy, your enterprise is likely to be affected. In the economic boom of the 1980s, many small-business owners thought their ventures were **recession-proof** and resistant to **downtrends** — lessening demands for products and services. To their dismay, these entrepreneurs found their sales eroded by the recession of the 1990s. Customers were suddenly retreating and cutting back on even the most essential products.

TIPS THAT SIGNAL ECONOMIC DOWNTRENDS

- Steady increase in the level of interest rates
- **Erosion of company profits**
- Lessening profits in competing companies
- Constant downward charting of **economic indicators,** for example, statistics that show wholesale prices or changes in transportation costs
- Falling off of customers, patrons, or clients
- Steady rise in accumulated business inventories
- Increase in articles in business journals and newspaper columns warning of recessionary indicators
- Increase in local unemployment

A regular analysis of the economic climate will enable you to foresee and prepare for downtrends and recessions (see the box above for some indicators of an economic downtrend). Many small businesses sink because they tend to stick with their original format and mode of operation; but you can stay afloat through a low business tide if you diversify or change your products and services in line with economic trends and consumer demands.

Ben & Jerry's is a fine example of a simple form of diversification. When Ben Cohen and Jerry Greenfield began formulating high-quality Vermont-made ice cream, they were successful enough that they could have continued marketing their initial products to a small contingent of loyal consumers. But they decided to expand by broadening their ice-cream line and diversifying into more far-ranging markets, including supermarkets. They also began adding related products, such as packaged gifts and cow sculptures, in their own company stores, since they already had the outlets and — most important — multitudes of repeat customers.

"Starting with a shoestring," commented a Vermont journalist in a local column, "they pretty soon added soles, heels, uppers, and boots."

Competitive Climate

As the owner of a successful small business, you must give continuing attention to the progress of your competitors. Evaluate the competition at three levels:

1. National, even though 99% of such companies are not direct competitors
2. Regional, where there may be a small percentage of interactive competition
3. Local, where the competition is direct and often quite strong.

These three factors together constitute the **competitive climate,** or the business atmosphere, which, like the weather, may fluctuate.

Sometimes it is bright, while at other times it is cloudy or downright miserable.

As your business grows, the effect of the competitive climate on it will change for the better or worse. In some cases, you might change the climate and improve your position relative to the competition for the better by taking certain calculated steps. Such steps might entail improving the quality of your product, revising your price scale, or offering a new product for which there is a growing consumer demand.

Every year of growth means that the stakes for your business are getting higher. The more profitable your business is, the more you stand to lose to the competition. In light of this, Paul Hawken, who founded a highly successful mail-order garden tool company, says, "You want to be the person who sets the stakes, not plays catch-up." If you follow the competition, he warns, most of your effort will have to be geared toward reacting to what competitors do. However, he says, "If you go your own way, set the standards, and keep looking forward, the majority of your creative energy goes into the ideas that promote new growth."

Hawken grew a part of his hand-tool business, not by undercutting the competition but by offering premium products. "The fact that our tools are 20 to 30 percent more expensive no longer looks like a cost but an investment," he explains, "because conventional tools wear out so quickly." He also sets the competitive stakes in two other ways: first, by backing his products unconditionally for life, and, second, by guaranteeing delivery to most locations within 24 hours.

Other ways of sidestepping the competition are:

- Phasing out lines of products that have saturated the market and replacing them with new products that are more in demand

- Restructuring prices for goods or services to be more competitive
- Consolidating the business with a major competitor to the mutual benefit of both organizations
- Being more aggressive in seeking prospective customers, patrons, or clients.

Demographic Climate

When you started your business, you determined in advance what the market was going to be for your products or services. You paid attention, in other words, to the **demographic climate,** the nature and make-up of the people with whom you intended to do business.

Demographics identifies the characteristics of a given population, according to various criteria, including sex, age, income, marital status, religion, ethnic background, race, and occupation. But these characteristics are not fixed; even after as little as one year, they may change, and they will continue to change. The population may increase or decrease; the birth rate may change; the economic standing of local residents may improve or worsen. The demographic climate can change gradually, for example, as young people are drawn to or away from a community. Or it can change abruptly, as in the case of a major plant shutdown that is immediately followed by a substantial rise in unemployment.

Changes in demographics take place in direct relationship to such factors as:

- The influx into the area of major industries that are recruiting employees from other regions
- Creation of retirement communities or other special-population developments, such as resort complexes, that change the age characteristics of the local population

- Marked changes in social attitudes, such as the acceptance of homosexuals or the idea of unmarried couples living together.

It is important for you to track these changes in your community as they affect the markets for your products or services. Here are some simple examples of positive reactions to demographic changes:

- As a southern town sees a steady influx of retired people who want to enjoy the warm climate, a cafeteria offers special discounts for seniors before 6:30 P.M.
- As a village in northern New England sees the arrival of more and more young people to enjoy new skiing facilities, the owner of a clothing store reacts by building a sporting goods annex at the foot of the slopes.
- As a small resort community in the Southwest reports a substantial rise in the per capita income of new home buyers, a paint and wallpaper store promotes a new home decorating service, with a focus on a luxury motif.

Climate of Risk

When you started your company, you may have identified all of the risk factors — at least those of any significance, such as a drastic weakening of the local economy, the arrival of a business rival too well heeled for you to compete with, or the possible loss of your major source of supply. But growth and expansion into new fields are more than likely to affect the risk factor. Understanding risk is vital for any owner of a small business. Equally important is **risk management** through such methods as insurance, improved security programs, and employee orientation. Hand in hand with growth should be a sound, realistic risk-reduction plan. You can refer to this as your **climate of risk**.

Your plan should include:

- A list of losses that can be expected annually, whether money, products, supplies, equipment, or other things important to business operations
- Risks that could result in these financial or physical losses
- Backup systems that can be called upon to reduce risks and losses, such as a contractual arrangement with an experienced consultant who can step in to assist in an emergency
- Special sales and/or consumer offers that can reduce risks at the twelfth hour, most commonly by reducing ungainly inventories and clearing space for new merchandise
- Consultations with specialists about areas of risk and ways to neutralize such hazards.

Insurance and the Reduction of Risk

When you started your company, one of your first steps was probably to make sure your new venture was adequately covered by insurance. But if your company is growing — and particularly if you foresee further expansion — the chances are that you have outgrown your original insurance needs. To make certain you now have adequate coverage, consider the following steps:

1. Reevaluate your original list of risks and risk factors.

2. Seek professional advice from a reliable insurance/risk consultant who is not connected with a private insurance agency.

3. Eliminate overlapping insurance that is adding to the cost but not to the degree of coverage.

4. Look for government protection, where appropriate. In regions subject to hurricanes, for example, private insurers cover wind damage, but government policies cover damage from flooding caused by storms.

5. Assign one person in your organization (if not you) to act as risk coordinator and stay abreast of change that could affect your coverage and security.

6. Reduce losses through better integrated inspection and safety programs, particularly in areas where risks may occur (such as a manufacturing plant where the odds for fires and personal injuries are likely to be higher than in an office).

7. Make sure that you or your risk coordinator is aware of premium reductions that are available if you can document improved safety records or a reduction in claims.

When reviewing potential risk factors and possible insurance coverage, many business owners find that it clarifies the situation to segment their requirements into three basic categories: essential coverage, non-essential but desirable coverage, and personnel coverage.

PART TWO

IMPLEMENTING ORDERLY GROWTH

CHAPTER FOUR

Financial Assistance for Development

KEY TERMS FOR THIS CHAPTER

balance sheet
break-even points
cash flow
equity capital
financial plan
financing
gross profit margin

gross volume
net volume
owner's equity
private lenders
Service Corps of Retired Engineers (SCORE)
short term

Small Business Administration
stock issues
term money
trade credit
valuing

Financing was one of the key factors you had to consider when you decided to go into business for yourself. Now it is time to ask yourself whether new financing or extended financing can help you to increase your business or expand it. You should view financing as a means to an end, such as improving the quality of your products or upgrading your services in order to meet changing customer demands.

A long-range financing plan is a vital element in assuring your company's growth. Martha Harding is a successful entrepreneur who, along with a partner, established clothing and furniture consignment shops in the Atlanta suburbs. They started with one shop, then added a second and a third, with the idea of

doubling the number by the end of the 1990s. Harding planned for additional financing to keep her business growing for the next two decades. "We expected we'd need additional financing at certain points along the line to accomplish our year-to-year objectives," she said, "yet each money-raising step was planned with the idea that the income produced would far exceed the cost of the financing."

Your Financial Plan

You undoubtedly developed a practical and realistic **financial plan** when you started your business. But now you must take an overview

CASH FLOW

In any small business, there is a continual increase and decrease in the **cash flow** and balance resulting from the normal functions of that business. The following diagram illustrates a typical flow of cash.

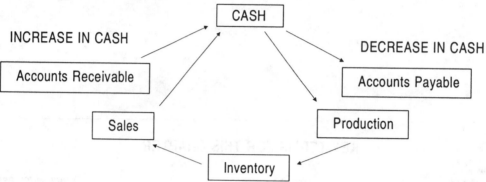

Cash is decreased in the acquisition of materials and the use of services needed to continue business operations. It is reduced when you pay bills, referred to as "Accounts Payable." When inventory is marketed and cash is generated, that is referred to as "Accounts Receivable." What you have to be alert to are changes in your cash flow resulting in your having too much or too little cash on hand. Such changes may indicate a need to review the input and output of cash for your business to remain financially healthy.

of your business, consider what effects growth has had on it from an economic standpoint, and then modify your basic financial plan to reflect these changes, whether they were anticipated or dictated by unforeseen circumstances. You should find it easier to prepare a financial plan now than when you were first planning your business, because you have realistic guidelines that have grown out of your own company's experience.

Your financial plan should include the following:

1. *Financial evaluations,* or brief conclusions about your business as it is now functioning, including:

- Economic health of the market
- Your position in that market
- Your **gross profit margin** during the years (or months) in business — the profits you bring in for goods and services before costs
- New or changing needs for equipment or supplies
- Payroll, taxes, and other key expenses.

2. *Profit-and-loss projections,* based on your record from the time the business started and continuing into the year ahead. This should be broken down into months so that any seasonal variations will be readily apparent. Projections for a full year should be sufficient, though some owners prefer to extend them for two, three, or more years.

3. *Sources of funds* — past, present, and future. This is meant to be a comparative financial inventory, to help you determine how much you needed to capitalize the business, how much you currently require to keep it going, and how much you will need in the future. The last evaluation should include all anticipated changes that will affect your capitalization needs.

4. *Pro-forma ("before-the-fact") balance sheet,* which is your estimate of your business assets, liabilities, and equity for the future. Based on your actual **balance sheet** from the past, you should be able to determine how much investment will be needed in the months to come as working capital for your business operations.

5. *Cash flow projection,* a working guideline to forecast the flow of cash into, and out of, your business during the year ahead. Prudent business management suggests that you keep no more cash on hand than is necessary to function without shortfall money emergencies. As in the above evaluations, use your past records as a basis for your projection.

Planning to Minimize Borrowing

According to the **Service Corps of Retired Executives (SCORE),** composed of managers who have been successful in many kinds of businesses, "Poor management is the reason why some owner-managers of small firms have trouble when they try to borrow. Those managers often fail to forecast and to plan for cash needs. The resulting business ailment is a 'cash crisis.' " "All too often," says John F. Murphy, a retired bank

executive and SCORE member, "the small business owner feels that his or her needs are financial when they are actually managerial."

With a long-range financial plan, you can often achieve your goal by borrowing only a nominal amount — far less than you may have originally anticipated on paper. Here is a case history of what was accomplished by the two owners of a firm that manufactured kitchen cabinets for a large real-estate developer. Awarded a contract to manufacture and install cabinets in a resort community, they were faced with a four-month deadline. They estimated that, in order to purchase materials quickly and hire extra labor, they would need extra working capital of about $60,000. By sharpening their pencils and using their negotiating and management skills, they were able to complete the work and meet their deadlines with a loan that was less than one-third of that amount. They achieved this through a financial plan composed of three elements:

1. An arrangement with their suppliers to ship and bill for their materials on a monthly basis over a three-month period

2. Securing an initial advance and then four monthly payments from the real-estate developer

3. An agreement not to draw any moneys from their business until cash flow balances were free and available.

The financial plan worked because there was never more than $15,000 (slightly less than the amount borrowed) in their accounts payable column during the period from the beginning of the job until its final acceptance. And by that time, they not only had enough cash on hand to repay the loan, but their profit as well.

Your financial plan need not be lengthy or complicated. Essentially, it is nothing more than advance bookkeeping — analyzing your records so that you can control, and often reduce, your costs. The following principles will be helpful:

• Make sure you know the nature of all of the common expenses in your business and how these relate to sales, inventories, the cost of goods sold, the cost of services rendered, gross profits, and net profits.

• Profits are at risk when your cost-control program is not effectively geared to sound marketing. A big sales volume does not necessarily result in a substantial profit.

• See where you can reduce costs without jeopardizing either the quality of products or the caliber of service.

• Analyze your expenses by using percentages rather than actual dollar amounts.

• Establish reliable break-even expense comparisons (the point at which gross profit equals expenses) to help establish a base for computation.

• Locate reducible expenses continuously by maintaining accurate profit-and-loss statements. Don't be content with annual (or even quarterly) P&L statements, at least not until you have established a very reliable pattern.

• When you locate a problem area regarding expenses and profits, focus on it and take corrective action immediately. You can refine the solution later, once you have determined the nature of the problem.

• Improve your inventory management to maintain a better balance of stock — keep enough on hand for efficient turnover, but not so much as to be glutted, or to risk stocking products and supplies that may become obsolete.

Financing for Growth

Your financial plan should reveal whether you will need to obtain outside sources of financing to help your business grow. But you may still have some concern about increased borrowing.

How far out on a limb can you go safely? To answer this, do some role playing. Put yourself in the position of a banker who is reviewing your application for a loan. You would insist on adequate and reliable financial data to prove that the business is solvent, profitable, and growing. The two fundamental financial statements that reveal these conditions are your balance sheet, the yardstick for solvency, and your profit-and-loss statement, a realistic indication of your money-making record.

Money lenders are particularly interested in the following data, all of which are reliable indicators of how much money you can commit your company to borrowing:

1. *Current Record Keeping.* Are your books in good condition regarding accounts payable and receivable, salaries, taxes, insurance premiums, employee benefits, and other monetary matters?

2. *Accounts Receivable.* Is there any evidence that some receivable figures are not exact, perhaps because of creditor commitments? Do you have substantial time lags in creditor payments or problems with cash reserves because of too many delinquent accounts?

3. *Inventories.* If you deal in merchandise, is it in readily marketable condition, with no markdown problems? Do you have proper supplies of raw materials on hand — enough to maintain production schedules without presenting storage problems or unnecessary cash outlays?

4. *Equipment and Other Fixed Assets.* Are these assets in good condition? Are your depreciation policies and schedules realistic? Have you made proper allowances for renewals and replacements of fixed assets when needed?

5. *Real Estate.* Are leases, mortgages, and other real-estate commitments reasonable and in line with comparable properties in your area? Do you have a regular, workable program for minimizing these expenses in the future?

CASH FLOW FORECAST FOR A SMALL BUSINESS

Pinpointing the timing of cash flows and the amounts of inflows and outflows can be as important as projecting profits for a growing business. Here is a worksheet, which you can adapt to your own needs.

CASH ACTIVITIES	MONTHS											
	1	2	3	4	5	6	7	8	9	10	11	12
SALES												
Less: Discounts												
Bad debts												
Labor												
Materials												
Leasing												
Overhead												
Commissions												
Waste												
GROSS PROFIT OR LOSS												
Less: Production costs												
Marketing costs												
Administration												
OPERATING PROFIT OR LOSS												
Less: Depreciation												
Interest												
Other costs												
PROFIT BEFORE TAXES												
LOSS BEFORE TAXES												
PROFIT AFTER TAXES												
LOSS AFTER TAXES												

Which Financing Option Is for You?

There are really only three kinds of basic financing: **short term, term money,** and **equity capital.** Short-term loans are borrowed for a brief period of time at a specified rate of interest. They are dissolved with a single payment or, at most, two to three payments. Term money is borrowed for a longer period and is paid back in installments; interest may be fixed or variable, and collateral is generally required. Equity capital is that portion of a business's capital that is furnished by stockholders.

You will want to keep in mind that the purpose of the money is the most important element in determining the kind of loan needed. It is vital, too, to analyze the repayment plan. A rule of thumb is that short-term loans can be paid from the liquidation of current assets, while long-term loans depend on earnings for their source of payment.

Here are some of the most common methods for financing a business that is already established and growing.

Loans through private lenders. Private lenders, such as banks, are the most common source because business owners usually have already established relationships with them. However, substantial time must be devoted to shopping around for the best rates. Consider short-term bank loans for purposes such as bolstering your accounts receivable balance for a period of one to three months, or for building your inventories over a period of up to six months. The latter option might be favorable for you, for example, if your business is seasonal and you have to stock up today in order to be ready for a rush of business tomorrow. Your best bet in such a case might well be to go to a bank whose loan officer is familiar with your operations and feels that your business anticipations are reasonable and realistic.

Loan assistance through the Small Business Administration. If you qualify, you may be able to obtain a "term" loan for a longer period through the **Small Business Administration** than would be possible with a commercial lender. However, you also will need more time for the application process and you will be subjected to more paperwork. According to *The ABC's of Borrowing,* published by the SBA, the agency's loan processors look at the following criteria:

1. The borrower's debt-paying record to suppliers, home mortgage holders, and other creditors
2. The ratio of the borrower's debt to net worth
3. The past earnings of the company
4. The value and condition of the collateral which the borrower offers for security.

In addition, the SBA loan processor will also look at your management ability, your character, and the future prospects of your business.

Stock issues. The advantage of **stock issues** is that you are spreading the economic risk among the stockholders. However, you may also be diluting your profits. In deciding whether to take this option, ask yourself one question: Do I want to relinquish some of the control I have over my business and forego some of the profit in order to avoid the financial commitments I would have to make to a bank or other lender?

Making plans for employees to own part of the business. This has a number of advantages, such as making your employees more enthusiastic about their work. But it also requires very detailed planning and coordination. As in the issuing of stock, this alternative weakens your administrative control over the company and lessens your share of the profits.

VALUATION WORKSHEET — ESTIMATES

	LAST YEAR	THIS YEAR	NEXT YEAR
Dollar figures:			
Gross income	_____	_____	_____
Net income	_____	_____	_____
Profits	_____	_____	_____
Number of employees	_____	_____	_____
Number of managers	_____	_____	_____
Sales force	_____	_____	_____
Loans outstanding	_____	_____	_____
Value of real estate	_____	_____	_____
Donations and good works	_____	_____	_____
Growth percentage, physical	_____	_____	_____
Growth percentage, monetary	_____	_____	_____
Other financial factors	_____	_____	_____
Intangible Values			
Rated: A+, A, B, C, D			
Standing in industry	_____	_____	_____
Standing in community	_____	_____	_____
Competitive position	_____	_____	_____
Public relations image	_____	_____	_____
Other intangible values	_____	_____	_____

This step is a promising one if you feel that the increased future earnings of your company will more than offset your loss in sharing the profits.

Merging with other organizations that have been successful. The results can be beneficial for both companies. The question to ask is whether you want to lose part of your identity in order to build an economic basis. A slightly different approach is to make a deal with one or more of your major suppliers in order to obtain what is known as **trade credit.** This type of money is not borrowed in the classic sense. Rather, it is money you owe suppliers who permit you to carry inventories on open accounts that will be settled later. This form of partial financing is appealing to suppliers who feel assured that the action will result in substantially increased sales for all concerned.

Selling off stagnating units of the business. If some parts of your business are not growing as expected, you might sell them off in order to obtain cash to expand other, more vigorous departments. Very few small businesses have the luxury of such a decision, but in some cases this approach has proven its worth. This kind of financing can also be achieved with equity funds. In this case, you relinquish some of your profits by selling an interest in your business to an investor.

Other options include realigning your investments and expanding the company's credit.

Valuing Your Business

Get in the habit of periodically **valuing** your business. If you prepare any kind of an annual report, you will have figures to use for comparison from year to year. Yet figures can be deceptive. They may look favorable, for example, if you have recently sold a segment of your business. But how do they look if you relate that sale to future growth and profits? You may have trimmed your sales force and thus reduced your monthly operating costs. But how will that decrease in your marketing power affect income during the coming months?

Valuing your business takes into account all of the factors that relate to profits, growth, increased customers, relationship to the competition, standing in your field or profession, and image in your community. Such an evaluation will also help you to decide whether it is advisable to consider new loans or other forms of underwriting to help your business grow further or to expand into new operational areas.

Remember the Financial Basics

Now that your venture is established and growing, don't make the mistake of assuming that you have a foolproof formula for success. This is the time when you should review the basics, carefully and thoughtfully. You will want to consider past results, as well as go through a checklist to see which areas are strong and which are weak.

FINANCIAL MANAGEMENT MISTAKES

From a financial standpoint, the growth of a small business, particularly if it is rapid or periodic, can often be as unfavorable as a long period of little or no growth. A substantial amount of profit can go down the drain because of mismanagement or confusion. Here are some common pitfalls:

- Incurrence of penalties or interest for late payment of bills
- Failure to have a plan for coping with delinquencies
- Excessive borrowing to counteract financial losses caused by inefficient billing practices
- Weak inventory management that results in surpluses, on one hand, or out-of-stock situations on the other
- Duplication of purchasing activities
- Failure to analyze market trends and credit systems
- Ignoring signs that portend financial futures.

WHAT IS YOUR BREAK-EVEN POINT?

The break-even point has been defined as that point in volume where enough units — whether goods or services or both — are sold so that the difference between selling price and the variable costs is just sufficient to cover the fixed costs. The break-even point for businesses differs widely, depending upon the nature of the business and the expenses and deductions that pertain to it. Each owner must determine realistically what that point is, considering all of the factors that can influence it.

Review the following points to help you zero in on your break-even point:

Gross income _____

Net income _____

Taxes and assessments _____

Accounts receivable _____

Accounts payable _____

Other liabilities _____

Fixed assets _____

Variable assets _____

Value of inventories _____

Other considerations _____

_____

_____

Here are some kernels of advice from *Your Small Business Made Simple* by Richard R. Gallagher that relate as well to an established and growing business as to a fledgling venture:

1. When estimating your operating costs, make sure that you do not overlook some of the less obvious ones that may be hidden in areas such as production, transportation, casualty losses, and recruiting.

2. When estimating your sales volume, take a close look at the **net volume** rather than the **gross volume,** to have a more realistic picture of your marketing potential.

3. Calculate the increase in taxes and various governmental fees and project these increases into the future.

4. Study your month-by-month estimate of cash flow.

5. Reevaluate your analysis of your company's **break-even point.** Make sure you understand not only what this figure was originally, but how much it has changed since going into business.

6. If you discover that you cannot break even without selling an unrealistically high number of items or providing an excessive amount of services, reassess your pricing structure, your customer credit plans, and your fixed costs to determine where things are out of line.

7. Calculate your **owner's equity** all over again. This relates to the properties you own,

the debts you owe, and the difference between them, all of which constitute your net worth. Your fixed assets can include land, buildings, furniture and fixtures, vehicles and transportation facilities, production equipment, and the like. But don't forget to allow for depreciation.

8. If you need refinancing, make a thorough study of all the options open to you before negotiating a loan or undertaking any other means of financial support.

9. Familiarize yourself with public organizations that can provide counsel and assistance, such as the Small Business Administration and SCORE (Service Corps of Retired Executives), at little or no cost.

10. Learn the pitfalls that can lead to refusals of loans or other financial aid. These include lack of planning, insufficient data, poor organization of a proposal, requests submitted to the wrong individuals or departments, and failure to acknowledge a weak credit history.

How to Manage Credit and Cash as Your Business Grows

Paying close attention to the details of financial management can have a significant impact on your bottom line. For instance, when you seek credit for your company, be sure you get the best interest rate possible. An experienced and well-qualified banker takes managers to task for overlooking this important issue. "Many managers just don't realize that money itself is a commodity," he said. "Like other products, it

ESTIMATED CASH FORECAST FOR A SMALL BUSINESS

	Jan	Feb	Mar	Apr	May	Jun	Jul	Aug	Sep	Oct	Nov	Dec
Cash in bank												
Petty cash												
Total cash												
Cash sales expected												
Other income												
Total receipts												
All Income												
Cash outflow												
Cash balance at month's end												

WHAT FURTHER FINANCIAL NEEDS DO YOU HAVE?

As you continue to grow, are you staying financially stable and meeting your obligations, as well as improving your profit-and-loss picture? Some points to check and keep in mind are:

Cash on hand _____
Cash elsewhere _____
Accounts receivable _____
Possible bad debts _____
Accounts payable _____
Possible discounts _____
Other liabilities _____
Value of inventory _____
Fixed assets:
    Land _____
    Structures _____
Variable assets:
    Equipment _____
    Vehicles _____
    Supplies _____
    Furniture and furnishings _____
Operational expenses:
    Salaries _____
    Commissions _____
    Other personnel costs _____
    Office _____
    Plant _____
    Utilities _____
    Advertising and promotion _____
    Communications _____
    Insurance _____
    Security _____
    Depreciation _____
Taxes and duties:
    Personnel _____
    Real property _____
    Commercial and business _____
    Carrying _____
    Other _____
Gross profits _____
Net profits _____
Losses _____

can be bought and sold for a price — what we refer to as interest rates. When business managers shop for much-needed equipment and supplies for their company, they do some homework and check out several stores of supply, as well as the quality of the merchandise they intend to purchase. When it comes to shopping for money, however, they overlook the fact that it is one of the most precious 'products' and resources available to any business, large or small."

The effective management of cash requires that you adhere to certain formulas and policies:

- Promptly deposit cash, checks, or other receivables in interest-bearing accounts
- Submit invoices consistently and without delay at about the same time each month
- Avoid idling money in non-yielding or low-yielding accounts, even for short periods of time
- Keep accounts receivable up to date

- Avoid borrowing in order to finance operations because of the slow collection of receivables
- Review all granting of credit to determine realistically the customer's ability to pay promptly
- Assess interest for accounts in arrears
- Establish practical procedures for dealing with slow or delinquent accounts
- Pay invoices promptly, preferably before the due dates, in order to maintain a favorable credit history
- Take full advantage of discounts offered by suppliers or contractors for cash or early payments
- Maintain effective communications with both creditors and customers, clearing the air promptly in all cases where there may be payment problems
- Make sure creditors understand the nature of your business and the seasonal or other problems that can disrupt your income and cash flow.

CHAPTER FIVE

The Evolving Tax Picture

KEY TERMS FOR THIS CHAPTER

accountability
certified public accountant (CPA)
corporation
depreciation
enrolled agent
excise tax

Federal Wages Taxes (FWT)
Federal Insurance Contributions
  Act (FICA)
import tax
intangible depreciation
partnership

recovery period
S corporation
sole proprietorship
tangible depreciation
tax attorney
taxation management

According to a national study by the Money Management Institute, when small businesses grow one of the most disturbing factors for the owners is the degree to which taxes may increase, thus eroding the anticipated profits. Often, managers completely overlook the tax implications of growth.

Tax Implications of Growth: Three Case Histories

Consider the following three examples* of small firms whose owners realized too late that the growth/tax relationship needed to be brought under stricter control:

* The names and some details have been altered.

• John and Alice Douglas, owners of The Pottery Place, started a cottage industry that was initially supplied by local artisans; later they added works from the state crafts association. As business grew, the Douglases began to carry pottery from other crafts associations, as well. That effort, too, was successful, and soon they decided to import large supplies of handcrafted pottery from other countries, notably Mexico, Costa Rica, and Ecuador. They reasoned that they could obtain products equal in artistry to their American-made lines, but at much lower cost. Since the new products could be sold at comparable prices, or even higher ones, by merchandising the "imported" factor, they stood to make a much greater profit. This rapid expansion of the business promised even greater growth and income — until the end of the year arrived, when the Douglases learned that importing goods put them in an entirely different tax classification than they had been in the year before. Now The Pottery Place was no longer a local cottage industry but an international organization. As such, it was subject to a state **excise tax,** a foreign **import tax,** and accumulated duties related to income following the sales of products from abroad.

The bottom line was a real jolt. Although the business had grown some 50 percent, the profits, when compared with the previous year, had dropped about 20 percent.

• Bright Lights, Inc., a small firm that manufactured lighting fixtures, found itself in an enviable position due to the convergence of two separate factors: demand increased and a local competitor went out of business. During a ten-month period, Bright Lights increased sales and almost doubled the number of its employees. The operating partners envisioned a rosy year-end picture, and an even rosier one for the future. But they were designers and engineers rather than financial planners, and they had left some financial-management decisions in the hands of unqualified subordinates in the billing and payroll departments.

At year's end, when an outside accountant arrived for his annual assessment of the books, he immediately spotted a costly oversight: Payroll deductions for the new employees had fallen far short of government regulations. A large proportion of the **Federal Wage Taxes (FWT)** and Social Security taxes under the **Federal Insurance Contributions Act (FICA)** had not yet been paid. The same was true of state and county deductions and taxes. Many weeks of very expensive review were required before the situation could be rectified, and the company suffered extensive penalties. These costs seriously diluted the profits and other gains expected from the company's growth and expansion. In addition, the com-

pany was placed on probation by federal and state authorities, which damaged its financial reputation and professional image.

• The Farm Ridge Construction Company had enjoyed five years of steadily increasing business, capped by a year in which it doubled its gross income in relation to the previous twelve months. According to the state tax laws under which the company functioned, it was responsible for carrying insurance to compensate employees for job-related injuries and illnesses attributable to working conditions (such as extreme cold or heat on construction sites and air laden with dust or chemical fumes). The company was also obligated to pay a county tax that provided certain forms of compensation insurance not otherwise covered by individuals or private companies.

The owners of the company had rashly committed themselves to many construction jobs that had been turned down by other firms in the business. These were high-risk ventures that threatened to cause work-related accidents and illnesses. The owners reasoned, however, that they were the kinds of contracts that called for premium payments and bonuses and thus increased the company's gross income.

Greed was tempered by what one critic of the management described as "just desserts" when the company was socked with greatly increased insurance premiums at every level and when the injuries escalated to such a point that the county upped the compensatory taxes by a large margin. As it turned out, because of the penalties and losses that management had failed to take into account, net income rose barely ten percent over the previous year — not much considering inflation and some additional costs of doing business.

By contrast, many other small businesses have experienced healthy growth without any significant increase in taxes, and in some cases with a lessening of taxes. Consider the case of

---

HOW TO MANAGE TAX WITHHOLDING

As you no doubt already know, the federal government and most state governments require that companies withhold from the paychecks of all regular employees a percentage of their earnings for income taxes. This money must be transferred to the proper government agencies regularly and promptly. For this purpose, employees are required to complete appropriate forms (such as the familiar W-4 Form, "Employee's Withholding Allowance Certificate").

The faster a business grows, the more often managers should review these withholding procedures, to make certain they are on target and the company will not be liable for penalties or interest. Withholding tax tables are available for computing the amounts in question.

The same holds true for withholding Social Security taxes under the Federal Insurance Contributions Act (FICA). Make certain that you have accurate information and records for all employees, and that the company's contributions correctly match those of the employees at the current FICA deduction rate.

Exotic Imports, Ltd., which was in the business of selling gift items from foreign countries. Its owners, fed up with the complications of constantly changing import taxes and duties, decided to "go American." They gradually phased out the imports, began selling only American-made products, and changed their name to Gifts & Gadgets, USA. Their tax burden was greatly abated.

The owner of another small company discovered that, by moving his office only 1.6 miles, he could do business in an adjacent state whose commercial taxes were about 30 percent less. Thus, he was able to remain in the same marketing area, yet commit fewer dollars to tax payments.

The Management of Taxation

If you already have a business that is successful and steadily growing, you already know that three great tax bites diminish your profits: federal, state, and local. Many owners of small companies accept this situation as the cost of doing business. **Taxation management**, however, involves more than simply paying them on time to avoid penalties and interest. It means learning how to make adjustments in your business plan in order to minimize your tax burden.

"Most of the company managers I have counseled," says Hardy Alister, who specializes in taxes for small businesses, "overpay taxes by anywhere from ten percent to as much as 35 percent."

How many times have you reviewed the tax situation and revised or updated your **accountability** — that is, the legal amount for which your company is indebted? This is a step that should be taken periodically, particularly if your business is growing, and preferably with the help of an expert. If you do not have an internal accountant who is thoroughly familiar with taxation, call in a **certified public accountant (CPA)**, **tax attorney**, or other professional. The cost of hiring a tax expert will be only a fraction of the money you will save by following his or her advice.

TAX WORKSHEET

Taxes for which a business owner can expect to be liable include: federal income tax, state income tax, municipal or other local tax, Social Security, federal unemployment, state unemployment, excise taxes, state sales taxes, local sales taxes, import taxes, property taxes, self-employment taxes, disability taxes, worker's compensation, local facility taxes (such as roads, sewage, and utilities), transportation taxes, and environmental taxes.

The following form can help you keep track of your tax liabilities. Use it as it is or modify it to create a tailor-made worksheet of your own.

TYPE OF TAX	DUE DATE	AMOUNT DUE	PAYEE, AND REMINDERS
FEDERAL TAXES			
Employee income tax			
Social Security tax			
Excise tax			
Owner-manager tax			
Corporation income tax			
Unemployment tax			
Import/export tariff			
Other taxes			
STATE TAXES			
Sales taxes			
Income tax			
Unemployment tax			
Franchise tax			
Environmental impost			
Other taxes			
COUNTY AND LOCAL TAXES			
Property taxes			
Sales taxes			
Real estate tax			
Licensing			
Other assessments			

The effective management of taxes is complicated and time-consuming, yet it is almost always well worth the effort. Here are some tips to help you stay on top of your tax situation:

1. Keep a running chart or calendar to pinpoint the dates on which taxes are due, their nature, and the amounts to be paid.

2. Establish communication with a reliable tax expert to whom you can turn for help, even if you have an experienced accountant on your payroll.

3. Keep a clipping and reference file of articles and news items on tax legislation that might affect your business, and support legislators who seem to be on your side.

4. Contact the Internal Revenue Service for a copy of its *Tax Guide for Small Business* (Publication #334).

5. Consider the tax benefits of changing your business structure from its present legal composition to another: sole proprietorship, partnership, corporation, or S corporation (see page 58 for a discussion of the S corporation).

6. Be alert to small-business tax situations that are the most frequently audited or hit with unfavorable decisions, such as overly high expense accounts or debatable philanthropic deductions.

7. Make sure you are handling employee tax withholdings properly and precisely, making adjustments and revisions promptly as the size or nature of your personnel roster changes.

8. Determine realistically the relationship between depreciation (see below) and taxation.

The Management of Depreciation

As your business expands, you should periodically consult with a tax specialist who is thoroughly familiar with your fields of operations and with the tax situation regarding all forms of **depreciation** that might be relevant, especially if you acquire any new form of commercial property, including equipment and buildings. Such property can be depreciated, affecting the total amount of business income that is subject to taxation. (Land, despite its classification as "physical property" and the fact that its value could be lessened by floods, landslides, or erosion, cannot be depreciated.)

Depreciation is divided into two categories:

1. **Tangible**, which includes buildings, plant equipment, furniture and furnishings, machinery, heating and air-conditioning, trucks and automobiles, outdoor structures, signs and the like. Land, however, despite its classification as physical property and the fact that its value could be lessened by floods or storms or erosion, cannot be depreciated.

2. **Intangible**, which covers such non-physical values as royalties, copyrights, patents, and franchises.

There are three fundamental requirements affecting a property being classified as depreciable:

1. The property must have a useful life of one year or more.

2. It must be vulnerable to wear and tear, obsolescence, corrosion or decay, loss of value through conventional and natural causes, or any other loss of effectiveness and utility.

3. It must be necessary for the conduct of the business or contribute to the generation of income.

The *IRS Tax Guide for Small Business* covers depreciation, as does IRS Publication #534, *Depreciation*.

The tax laws call for varying periods of depreciation, depending on the nature and age of the property that is being claimed. For example, you will find that the depreciation period, or the **recovery period**, for trucks and automobiles is three years; for furniture, fixtures, and equipment, five years; for buildings and other real property, 15 years. However, these tax codes are always being revised, so you must

---

YOUR SECRET TAX PREPARERS

The least-known type of tax preparer is the **enrolled agent,** a specialist who has been serving Americans in tax matters for over one hundred years.

What are enrolled agents? They are experts certified by the Treasury Department to represent their clients in hearings before the Internal Revenue Service or related agencies. There are some 30,000 enrolled agents in service today. Some have been previously employed by the IRS for at least five years, while others have been certified after passing a comprehensive government test covering federal taxation and comparable matters.

If you need a specialist in tax preparation or have complex questions about taxation for small businesses (or your own personal filing), an enrolled agent can set you straight and guide you in using tax laws to your advantage. Fees are reasonable, ranging from about $75 to $300 per return, depending upon the complexity of the entries and the number of forms that have to be prepared.

To locate a qualified enrolled agent, ask business friends knowledgeable about taxation to suggest one; see if your state has a Society of Enrolled Agents; or call the IRS.

---

refer to current classifications and recovery periods before making any claims on tax returns.

Legal Structures vs. Tax Structures

If your firm's operations are running smoothly, you probably have no cause to change its legal structure. However, the owners and managers of many small companies do make a switch when they find their businesses growing, and there can be certain advantages in doing so. Tax structures play an important role in decisions affecting legal structures under which a company's management elects to do business.

Here are some of the tax advantages and disadvantages inherent in the three legal structures designed for small businesses:

The Sole Proprietorship. A sole proprietorhip is defined as a business owned and operated by one individual, which can be started after obtaining whatever necessary licenses are required for local businesses.

Advantages: It offers relative freedom from government control and special taxation.

Disadvantages: The individual proprietor is fully responsible for taxes, which could adversely affect personal income tax obligations if not properly handled. Taking deductions for business expenses is permissible, of course, but can often be tricky and may trigger a tax audit.

The Partnership. A partnership is defined as "an association of two or more persons to carry on as co-owners of a business for profit."

Advantages: It offers relative freedom from government control and special taxation.

Disadvantages: The firm can be bound by the acts of one partner. Thus dishonesty or misman-

LAWS AND REGULATIONS THAT AFFECT YOUR BUSINESS

The growth of your business has implications not only in terms of taxes but also in regard to certain government laws and regulations. Familiarize yourself with the following regulations. Mark the ones that are applicable to your business and note the reasons why. These are federal regulations for the most part but can tie in with local legislation as well. (They are listed alphabetically, not by priority.)

Age Discrimination in Employment Act _____

Civil Rights Act _____

Clayton Act _____

Consumer Credit Protection Act _____

Consumer Products Safety Act _____

Employee Retirement Income Security Act _____

Equal Credit Opportunity Act _____

Equal Employment Opportunity Act _____

Equal Pay Regulations _____

Fair Credit Billing Act _____

Fair Credit Reporting Regulations _____

Fair Debt Collection Regulations _____

Fair Labor Standards Act _____

Fair Packaging and Labeling Act _____

Federal Trade Commission Act _____

Federal Wages and Hours Regulations _____

Federal Warranty Regulations _____

Fibrous Materials Regulations _____

Flammable Fabrics Regulations _____

Food, Drug, and Cosmetic Act _____

Hazardous Substances Regulations _____

National Labor Relations Regulations _____

Natural Materials Regulations _____

Occupational Safety and Health Act _____

Pure Food and Drug Act _____

Robinson-Patman Act _____

Sherman Antitrust Act _____

Social Security Regulations _____

Wheeler-Lea Act _____

agement by one partner could adversely affect the welfare of all other partners; these effects might include excessive tax liability.

The Corporation. By far the most complex of the three business structures, the **corporation** is a specific legal entity, distinct from the individuals who own or manage it.

Advantages: Employees and officers are not personally responsible for the tax obligations of the company, even if serious delinquencies occur.

Disadvantages: Tax reporting is much more complicated than for sole proprietorships or partnerships and can adversely affect the profit/loss picture if not properly managed. Corporations are affected by many more kinds of taxes than other business structures, and the nature of these taxes requires serious decisions about such matters as joint ventures, location, securities, and management.

The S Corporation

If your business is growing or changing, you might want to consider becoming an **S corporation.** The advantage is that as an individual you are less liable for any tax delinquencies (as well as other kinds of losses) suffered by the business.

An S corporation can be established only if it meets certain restrictions. It must be a domestic company, for example, can issue only one classification of stock, can have no more than 35 shareholders, and can have no shareholders who are non-resident aliens.

CHAPTER SIX

Growing on the Computer

KEY TERMS FOR THIS CHAPTER

computer programmers
hardware
primary data
secondary data
service bureau

software
spreadsheet analysis
time-sharing
upgrading
word processing

The National Federation of Independent Business found that computer use by small businesses increased at a rate of more than ten percent a year, on average, in the early 1990s. This change can be attributed to two important factors: first, the decreasing cost of computer systems, called **hardware,** and their related programs, called **software;** and second, increasing sophistication and familiarity with computers on the part of small-business owners. For companies that have been successfully growing for a period of two or three years or more, computerization has become almost mandatory for continued growth and the maintenance of their competitive position.

If you feel it is time to computerize many of your company's systems but are confused by the great variety of computers and electronic data systems on the market, don't despair.

Many suppliers offer reliable consultation at no charge. In addition, according to the Small Business Administration, "These companies provide a good source of information on general descriptions of particular management techniques, as well as help on specific management problems."

Indeed, it is in the efficient application of computer programming to management that small businesses are still facing problems. For example, when IBM completed some surveys on the use of computers by small businesses for routine applications, it found that only 14 percent used their systems for payroll functions, and that only half of the small firms with computer installations used them for any advanced operations.

The case of an energy company in Pennsylvania illustrates the errors some small-business owners make in computerizing their operations. After investing almost $50,000 in computer systems, the president of the company fired his computer programmers and turned to packaged software programs on topics relating to his field of operations. But he was only partially successful. The commercial producers of software may be very knowledgeable about certain kinds of business requirements that apply across the board. But they cannot be expected to program the complex details of a very specialized business into their software.

Elbert Downs, a manufacturer of automotive parts with several small plants in Ohio, has used computers and software effectively for almost two decades. "From the time we placed our first hardware in operation," he recalls, "I explained to everyone concerned that this equipment was going to facilitate production, inventory filing, quality control, and related functions. But, I added, computers could not be expected to help us with very specialized technical functions — at least not until we were able to program them to do so."

Successful Computer and Software Applications

Computers cannot create order out of chaos, but with careful planning and selection of the right hardware and software, many of the functions of your business can be performed more efficiently through electronic data processing.

Evaluating Your Needs

Before you even venture out to shop for a computer, clarify your needs. Take a piece of paper and list all aspects of your business that might benefit from computerization — such as bookkeeping, inventory control, the manufacture of products or parts, accounts receivable and payable, research and development, personnel records, and marketing.

Then prioritize which divisions, departments, or functions of your firm seem to be most in need of attention and assistance. If an operation is proceeding smoothly, give it less priority than an operation that has a record of problems and erratic performance.

Consider, too, the managers and supervisors in charge of these departments and how well qualified they might be to manage an electronic data-processing system. Ask yourself whether possible performance improvements are likely to justify not only the cost of equipment, but a training program and the possible addition of personnel, such as **computer programmers** or maintenance specialists.

Finally, consider the short-term services of a consultant. Salespeople will be able to answer only very basic questions about the products and services they promote. A consultant will be able to evaluate your needs and help you find the most suitable and reliable equipment. The cost will not be great, especially if you can enlist the aid of a manufacturer who views you as a prospective long-term customer.

Let Software Be Your Guide

As consumers, we are accustomed to buying hardware — cameras, radios, cassette players, automobiles, washing machines, and other equipment. We are seldom concerned with what goes into them to produce the end results, such as films, tapes, fuel, or detergents. When it comes to computers, it is not difficult to locate reasonably priced hardware with the capabilities to perform most of the functions demanded by small-business operations. But software is of paramount importance. Take heed of the advice of one expert, "Purchasing the machine is secondary to finding the best program for your particular application."

Software is defined as a set of practical instructions designed to result in a planned operation for a specific goal. Software for the preparation of this book, for example, might direct the hardware (the computer) in establishing the layouts and spacing of texts, the spelling of words, and grammatical usage. Software for the inventory control of a retail business might keep a running account of several thousand products and parts, providing instant information about the numbers on hand, locations, prices, and code numbers. Other programs perform specific applications such as accounting, **spreadsheet analysis,** and **word processing.**

Software is available to help you manage the following types of information:

- General business data on such subjects as employee recruiting and management, marketing, taxation, bookkeeping, inventory management, payrolls, cost control, sales forecasting, and customer servicing
- Specialized data relating to the business itself, in areas such as research, technology, and industry forecasting
- Projections of costs for ongoing research or sales and marketing programs, and other projects
- A regular updating of data that change seasonally, geographically, or during fluctuations in the industry's economy.

Replacing Hardware, Upgrading Software

If you have already been using a computer in a limited way and are afraid you are outgrowing it as your business expands, you may simply need

more advanced and extensive programming, rather than new hardware. However, it may be necessary to replace existing hardware if you have one or more of the following problems:

- There is not enough hardware for all of the departments or functions you would like to see computerized
- The processing is too slow for current demands on time and data
- Existing equipment cannot effectively be coordinated with new hardware being installed
- Data storage capabilities are limited
- The manufacturer has gone out of business and parts, supplies, and service are difficult to obtain.

If none of these problems are plaguing your operation, you probably can attain your objectives by enlarging, improving, or supplementing your software programs. Software producers are constantly updating and **upgrading** their wares, issuing new versions of various programs with improved capabilities. If you are a steady customer, your supplier should offer two benefits to you: discounts for improved software programs; and low-cost updates to complement existing programs.

As your business grows, continue to reevaluate your software needs. Do you want software that is faster? Covers a wider range of operations? Has greater storage capacity? Performs functions not currently available to you? Requires less storage space? Is more durable when exposed to extremes of heat, humidity, and vibration? If so, ask your suppliers what they can do for you.

Service Bureaus

When considering your data processing needs, ask yourself whether you need in-house capabilities or whether a **service bureau** could handle this aspect of the business for you on a contractual basis.

The answer depends on a number of considerations, among them:

- The extent of your data-processing needs
- The comparative costs of in-house vs. outside processing
- The availability of reliable outside services
- The availability of qualified specialists to employ in-house
- The degree to which you foresee the expansion of your business in the future.

If you have not already invested in electronic data-processing equipment, you would do well to investigate service bureaus in your area. Through these bureaus, your records — such as payrolls, accounts receivable and payable, inventories, financial statements, periodic reports, bank records, and other constantly changing business data — can be computerized. The only work required of you or your department managers is to deliver data and documents to the bureau at regularly stated intervals.

For this kind of service you will be charged a one-time basic fee, ranging from a few hundred dollars to two thousand dollars, for designing a program that meets your requirements. At the low end of the price scale is a standard package system designed by the bureau to accommodate small businesses that are conventional in nature. At the high end is a specially designed program, tailored to the needs of an enterprise that has particular, or unusual, requirements.

Thereafter, you will pay a service fee of several hundred dollars each month as a processing charge. You are at liberty, generally, to cancel the program with 30 days notice. Most programs are flexible enough that you can ask the bureau to make changes, additions, and modifications at a later date for a modest charge.

The Association of Data Processing Service Organizations can provide you with more information on service bureaus. (See *Resources.*)

Time-sharing

You can also take advantage of a common data-processing arrangement known as **time-sharing.** The term refers to a system whereby one organization owns and operates computer hardware and installs terminals on the premises of its customers. These terminals are connected by telephone cables to the main computer and can generally be operated by employees with only a basic understanding of electronic data processing. The system is ideal for any business that needs a computer periodically or intermittently, but not on a full-time basis. Such an arrangement has the following advantages:

- Very small installation cost
- Low to moderate rental charges
- No problems with shut-downs or repairs
- Limited training requirements
- The flexibility to increase or decrease use without monetary penalties.

Orientation and Training

A computer study by the National Federation of Independent Business revealed that the most commonly mentioned problem was the need for far more employee training than had been anticipated. In one typical case cited by the American Management Association, a financial analyst who usually required about six hours to prepare a monthly report, *B.C.* (Before Com-

---

COMPUTER FRAUD

During orientation sessions and training programs, stress the fact that employees who work with hardware and software not only have increased responsibilities but ethical obligations not unlike those of personnel who handle cash and other valuables. As use of computers increases, so do reports of computer-assisted fraud and embezzlement. Users who know their electronic systems intimately can manipulate computers and extract confidential information.

The United States General Accounting Office disclosed that most computer-related crimes result from preparation of false input data to computer-based systems. You can avoid being victimized by this kind of crime by establishing controls that monitor input and alert you to abnormal changes in operation.

---

puters), was spending almost triple that amount of time when "aided" by a computer. In another instance, the misuse of computer programming resulted in almost 90 hours of lost time in an engineering department because the wrong software had been used.

Your computer training program should be compatible with all other educational programs offered by the company. The following steps should guide you to one that is effective and reasonable in regard to time and cost:

1. Determine which departments or functions involve employees who need further information about computer installations.

2. Identify the procedures by two categories: first, basic training, and second, continuing orientation and updating.

3. Segment the programs further into two classifications: hardware and software.

4. Establish specific objectives for employees who participate.

5. Organize the curriculum so subject matter is outlined in order of sequence and priority.

6. Schedule the training sessions so they occur during normal business hours and at times that do not conflict with the regular duties of the participants.

7. Offer classes outside of business hours only on a voluntary basis for employees who see this as an opportunity to advance themselves.

8. Select instructors carefully, based as much on their teaching skills as on their knowledge of the subjects at hand. Use staff instructors if they are competent; otherwise seek outside help.

9. Consult the suppliers of your equipment and systems for advice.

10. Formulate practical tests to qualify participants and consider issuing certificates or other evidence of satisfactory completion.

A professor who teaches electronic data processing (EDP) at the college level has another ingenious suggestion for small companies who have new computers but don't know how to use them to full capacity. "Hire college students, like the ones I have in my courses, to work in your offices during spring breaks and summer vacations. They haven't been hog-tied by the old conventional data-compilation systems, they are at home with electronics, laser printers, and accessories like the mouse, and they think of the computer as a jolly good game. In no time at all, they can provide guidance for older office employees and get them

BOOKKEEPING YESTERDAY, TODAY, AND TOMORROW

A review of past performance is a practical way of evaluating your bookkeeping system. If the procedures and methods you established when you first went into business have caused no problems in the operation of your company, the chances are that they are fundamentally sound. Any changes required are likely to be more a matter of degree than approach. But this is a good time to make comparisons and evaluate your books, chronologically and by category. You can accomplish this by selecting three key dates in the history of your company and completing the following review for each. The first date might be your company's first anniversary. The second might be a midpoint in its history. And the third might be records that are current, or close enough to be reliable today.

The key elements to examine and compare on a month-to-month and year-to-year basis are the following:

Assets

List everything of value that is owned by the business, but also anything that is legally due the business and feasible to collect.

Total assets include all net book values, which are the amounts derived by entering the acquisition price of the assets and then subtracting carrying charges, depreciation, or arrears that probably will not be received as cash.

Current Assets

List cash and resources that could be readily converted into cash within 30 to 60 days with little or no financial penalties. Besides cash on hand or in accessible bank accounts, current assets include:

- Accounts receivable, the amounts legally due from customers and clients in payment for merchandise or services
- Inventory, which includes products that are finished, work in progress, raw materials, and supplies
- Temporary investments, such as holdings that generate interest or dividends and could be converted into cash within the calendar year. You should also include stocks, bonds, certificates of deposit, and other marketable securities. List their market values as of the historical company dates you are using for comparisons.
- Prepaid expenses, for equipment, office supplies, furnishings, leases, rentals, and even insurance.

Long-term Investments

Also referred to as long-term assets, these are holdings that your business expects to retain for at least one year and that typically yield interest or dividends. In this category, include stocks, bonds, and special savings accounts. Be careful, however, not to duplicate any entries you have listed under the "Temporary investment" category above.

Fixed Assets

Under this category, list land, real estate, plant equipment, and other resources you have acquired for your operations and do not intend to sell right away. Use original purchase prices, less depreciation (if any) as of the dates you are using for comparisons. If you have leased any fixed assets to others, make note of the sums and legal agreements.

Additional Assets

You may have assets that do not fit any of the above categories, which are on hand during the given dates. These could be tangibles, like scrap metal with a sale value, or intangibles like trademarks and royalties that have monetary value to prospective purchasers.

Liabilities

The bookkeeping values here relate to obligations payable within whatever cycle of operations you select for your comparisons, particularly the following:

- Accounts payable, amounts owed to your suppliers of merchandise, supplies, or services
- Short-term notes, the balances due to pay off short-term debt for borrowed funds
- Current portions of long-term notes, due on notes whose terms exceed 12 months
- Interest payable, including any accrued fees for use of both short-term and long-term borrowed capital and credit extended to your business
- Taxes payable, in the amounts estimated or paid on the comparative dates you selected
- Payrolls, owed but not yet paid on the dates selected

Equity

Also referred to as net worth, this is the claim of the owners of a business as to the worth after valid deductions for withdrawals by partners or other principals, or the issuance of dividends or bonuses.

Total Liabilities and Equity

The sum you compute here for these two amounts should always match the sum for Total Assets.

into the technology, as well as the spirit of keyboard manipulation."

You and your key managers would do well to purchase personal computers (PCs) for use in your homes. A PC is a handy accessory for the running of any household, but more important, it will help you to feel more comfortable with the use of hardware and software alike. Publications on training and orientation are also available, as well as literature from the manufacturers of hardware and the producers of software.

Types of Data

Whether you have your own computer, use a service bureau, or participate in a time-sharing system, your business will tap two different kinds of resources. The first, which is vital for a growing enterprise, is referred to as **primary data.** This includes facts relative to a subject field that are not readily available in standard sources of data — either within a company and industry or outside of them. Such data may require a considerable amount of time, and often initiative, to locate. New research on a subject and unusual data that do not fit conventional classifications are some examples of primary data.

The second resource is known as **secondary data,** and includes information normally available through conventional sources such as the federal government, the local chamber of commerce, or a data service. Common subjects are sales figures, market forecasting, inventory control, training programs, payroll confirmations, expense accounts, insurance claims, medical records, equipment depreciations, and accidents or casualties.

Expanded Bookkeeping

It goes without saying that the growth and expansion of an organization will increase bookkeeping demands, often bringing new challenges to management, as well as escalate the time and effort needed to maintain adequate records. If you have a computer, or access to one through time-sharing, routine

---

BOOKKEEPING AND RECORD-KEEPING CHECKLIST

As your business grows, review the following subjects, even though you may have done so in detail when your business was first established:

- How long to keep records for business and tax purposes
- Expense management
- The qualifications of your bookkeeper(s) as the business expands
- Measurement of present progress
- Review of compliances with government regulations and company policies
- Study of ways to use ratio analysis (the computation of current assets and liabilities, net sales, net worth, total debt, and net profit) for information and decision-making.

bookkeeping — and even specialized record keeping — will be that much easier and quicker.

Keeping books in proper and sequential order is essential to the effectiveness of your accounting system. If you do not have an experienced bookkeeper on your payroll, you should arrange to hire one on a part-time or consulting basis. Even if you are knowledgeable about bookkeeping, it pays to have an objective opinion and the periodic services of a professional who keeps current on procedures, accountability, and regulations.

The Small Business Administration recommends that you maintain the following five fundamental kinds of records:

1. Cash receipts
2. Cash disbursements
3. Accounts receivable
4. Sales records
5. Sales tax, and related, payments.

CHAPTER SEVEN

Growing Pains: Space Needs and Location

KEY TERMS FOR THIS CHAPTER

affiliated business district

regional mall

shopping center

specialty products

store layout

theme mall

trading area

traffic flow

The physical and material needs of a company that offers substantially more goods and services than it did in the past deserve as much attention as sales, marketing, production, and other major operational needs. People who are creative and productive particularly need a certain amount of freedom in order to contribute their imagination and skills to company projects. And freedom includes enough breathing space in which to function.

Recognize the need to grow along with your business. Begrudging adequate space is a misguided method of cost-cutting. The noted business writer, Raymond Dreyfack, in his book, *Sure Fail: The Art of Mismanagement*, refers to it as "cupidity stupidity."

Analyzing Your Space Needs

When considering spatial matters and expansion, ask yourself the following questions, and consider the potential advantages to your business that are noted.

• *Should I make additions to the structure(s) in which my business functions?*

If the buildings are structurally sound and pleasant enough in design, such additions might be far more economical than other alternatives. Don't hesitate to sound out your employees on how they feel about the place in which they work. After all, familiarity with their surroundings can have an important supportive effect on their work.

- *Should I move all, or part, of the business to one or more new buildings?*

Cost is the most significant factor here. Yet if you try to skimp on cost by moving only part of the business, ultimately you could end up paying more if you weaken lines of communication and scatter your departments or operations.

- *Do our storage or warehousing facilities need expansion to allow for better stock control?*

Since storage space is generally the cheapest kind of footage, it is wise to have enough of it to avoid complications. Determine, too, whether you want more vertical space, more horizontal space, or a combination of both. If you have a growing proportion of dead storage, consider whether some of it might be scrapped or sold.

- *Should we relocate to a different region entirely, in order to obtain more space at less cost per square foot?*

A good idea, if the cost differentials are substantial. But before moving, make sure you have accurate comparisons of all other factors (such as local taxes and the availability of supplies) that will inevitably effect the cost of doing business. (See page 73 for a full discussion of changing location.)

- *Have we been taking physical inventories regularly to determine areas of obsolescence?*

Space, like everything else, has a certain life span, a factor many managers are likely to forget. If certain blocks of space don't seem to be paying their own way, revitalize them so they are put to better use.

- *Does inadequate space restrict employee performance and efficiency?*

If you put two employees in a space that was formerly occupied by one, you may save a little bit on the real-estate ledger. But you may also decrease individual productivity. And don't overlook the relationship of space to morale.

- *Do we have enough exterior space for parking, transportation, and employee recreation?*

Exterior space is generally cheap, so you can afford to be generous in allocating more of it to the benefit of employees. To be able to park quickly, easily, and with minimal exposure to bad weather is high on the priority list of employees. So is the availability of a recreation area — even for those who seldom use it.

- *Is there a person or committee regularly in action to evaluate spatial needs and problems?*

Unless you just love to wrestle with the problem yourself, delegate this important aspect of business to someone else.

- *What is the actual cost of adding space in relationship to improved production or income, and how would this be financially beneficial?*

Sharpen your pencil and get to the bottom line. It is not always easy to relate space to improved efficiency or increased earnings and profits. However, by keeping accurate records and making comparisons with other companies in your field, you can generate figures and data that will be meaningful.

Space Adjustments: Two Case Histories

- The owner of the Broad Creek Manufacturing Company in northwestern North Carolina had a severe space problem when his company grew from a $5 million business in 1987 to more than double that within four years. He owned four main buildings — an office, a warehouse, a production facility, and a transportation garage. Rather than commit himself to the expense and effort of major construction, he brought in an architectural engineer to reevaluate the existing space. It was easy to see that the space squeeze was largely confined to the production plant, primarily because of the increasing numbers and types of parts being manufactured.

WORKSHEET FOR THE ALLOCATION OF SPACE

This form will help you outline alternatives for improving the use of space for employees, operations, production, and other essentials.

Space Used For	Current Space	Amount Needed	Future Plans
Headquarters			
Office Management			
Accounting			
Meetings			
Departments:			
(1)			
(2)			
(3)			
(4)			
Production			
Personnel			
Storage			
Advertising			
Marketing			
Transportation			
Security			
Training			
Cafeteria			
Rest Room			
Recreation			

In the end, the production plant was moved to the warehouse, a much larger structure. Warehouse paperwork was transferred to the office building, where computerization had decreased the need for extensive filing space, and an assembly and packing line was repositioned in the transportation garage where it in fact operated more efficiently.

This kind of solution is not always possible. However, it brings home the point that you should always evaluate your growing space problems carefully — and creatively — before you make any drastic additions.

• A small advertising agency had just taken on a new, multi-million-dollar client. That was the good news. The bad news was that, as a result of the new business, the copy chief had to accommodate three new copywriters within the space currently allocated to six. The copy chief's two options did not seem at all satisfactory: either to make nine much smaller offices in the same overall space, or to pair off two writers in each of the three largest offices.

Knowing the complaints he would have about privacy and difficulty concentrating from those who were forced to double up, the copy chief came up with a third alternative. His idea was to eliminate an adjacent storage area, add that to the space occupied by the six existing offices, and make nine that were ample in size and would permit each writer to work in privacy and quiet.

What about the supplies now housed in the storage area? Quite simple. These were for the most part little-used films, archives, and past records that had to be retained for a few years before being destroyed. Classified in nine specific categories, they were easily relocated to shelves and cabinets in the nine new offices that emerged from the copy chief's ingenious plan.

They required less space than a second human occupant, and of course, were hardly likely to disconcert copywriters trying to concentrate on their creative assignments.

Suggestions about Layout

You may not have realized it as your business evolved and underwent subtle, but steady, changes, but you may need to reorganize your internal traffic and space layouts to improve operational efficiency. Ask yourself these questions, in light of the accompanying suggestions:

• *Do we have the right types and amounts of space for traffic flow in hallways, stairs, elevators, ramps, and escalators? Do these facilitate or hamper the movement of people, products, and supplies?*

Bear in mind that your needs are completely different when you compare space for people and equipment *in motion* with space for those same elements *at rest.*

• *Have we planned our layouts to take care of any future expansion or changes in operations?*

Whenever you make significant changes of any kind, your plans should include built-in adjustments to take care of as many future needs as possible with minimal cost. Architectural engineers are trained to expect that basic changes will be needed within five to ten years after completing almost any commercial project.

• *Are our storage and warehousing areas not only adequate but in the right locations for effective use and movement?*

The lowest item on any list of spatial and locational priorities is likely to be storage. We are brought up with the notion that you store things in the attic, the cellar, in the rafters or the garage — just about anywhere that is difficult to reach and useless for any other purpose. Unfortunately the same outlook has pervaded the business world. Take a second look at your storage and warehousing areas and consider whether they should be upgraded to improve your overall efficiency.

• *Are operational functions, from the handling of mail to the flow of production and assembly lines consistent with our needs?*

If these functions have been handled "the same old way" since you've been in business, the chances are that they need serious rehabilitation.

• *Are the relationships of offices, departments, and personnel facilities logical and practical, or should these be shifted?*

The more your business has grown, and the more quickly it has blossomed, the greater the need will be for a review and possible relocations of your various company departments.

SPACE AND PSYCHOLOGY

An ample amount of space results in favorable impressions that can ultimately affect your business in a positive way. Ample space can:
- Improve your corporate image
- Suggest reliability and competence to clients and customers and others who visit your premises
- Make employees feel more comfortable and enthusiastic about coming to work
- Enhance your employee recruiting program
- Attract investors, who often judge appearance as a sign of success
- Strengthen your authority and that of your associates by generating the respect that comes with managing in a prosperous looking atmosphere
- Provide a more flexible environment in which you can shift offices, add a conference room, or start a new department on a trial basis without additional cost
- Allow you to present a visible award to managers who have performed well by giving them larger offices.

Transportation and Space

If your organization requires a considerable amount of transportation for merchandise, supplies, or personnel for its day-to-day operations, consider this an element of space that has to be managed. Do you have enough truck space to haul goods promptly and without breakage, and enough passenger vehicle space to transport people safely and comfortably? If you cut or restrict transportation space and capability, you may be throttling one of your most important sources of production and income.

Raw materials are often a factor in determining spatial needs and company location. "Mark the sources of your raw materials with pins on a large map," suggests Fred I. Weber, Jr., author of a business treatise, *Locating or Relocating Your Business*. "If they all come from one area, you should consider what advantages a competitor located adjacent to the source has

over a more remote facility. It may be more important to be closer to raw materials than to your customer, or vice versa." He suggests that you ask yourself the following questions:
- Are there facilities to bring the raw materials in rapidly and economically?
- Can you always be assured of a supply regardless of the season?
- Does the supply of raw materials from the area seem assured for the foreseeable future?
- Should you plan on an alternate source which might affect your planned location?
- Will the cost of raw materials from the present source change dramatically in the future?

Why Change Location?

Most small companies, whether in manufacturing or retail, were initially established in their locations for specific, usually positive, reasons.

It is vital, for example, for small manufacturing businesses to be located near their markets if they want to be competitive with larger corporations that can afford a network of supply systems to numerous points of sale. Other small producers may determine that they can be most efficient if they locate near the source of raw materials, or where energy is cheap or experienced employees are readily available. Any company that relies heavily on power, such as a firm in the field of metals processing, must evaluate haulage and storage costs (now and in the future) very carefully. The transportation charges for coal, for example, are astronomical and are therefore an important factor in plant location.

An evaluation of companies in the field of retailing suggests the following points in regard to location:

1. Locate the business where the **traffic flow** is strong and steady and prospective customers are plentiful.

2. Avoid locations where business tends to be seasonal.

3. A mail-order business should be located in an area where shipping costs are low and there is a surplus of part-time help available at modest hourly wages.

4. Locate where there is an active need for your products and services, but competition is weak.

5. Location can be more flexible for the **specialty products** field because customers are willing to go out of their way to purchase items not carried by other kinds of retailers.

The mere fact that your business has grown in size does not necessarily mean that you must now change your location. Yet there are times when a move should be evaluated as a means of contributing to future growth and/or improving the profit picture. There might be factors specific to your business or changes in the neighborhood around you that might indicate that a move is in order. Among the most common indicators in favor of change are:

Local Factors

• The influx of crime into the area

• A lessening of available resources and services in the present location

• A steep increase in local taxes or commercial assessments

• Lack of suitable land for future expansion

• Cutbacks in mass transportation or access roads

• Decline in the quality of local emergency services, such as fire and police protection and ambulance or rescue squad operations

• Population shifts that make future employee recruitment difficult or more costly.

Specific Factors

• Overcrowding in a building that cannot be readily enlarged, economically or structurally

• Dispute with a landlord over terms of a lease renewal

• Decision by the owner to move residence to a distant location (usually in the case of a very small business or cottage industry)

• Merger with another organization whose facilities in another area are more suitable for the joint venture

• Shift in the market for the firm's products or services

• Inroads of a major, aggressive competitor.

Determining When and Where to Move

Your business seems to be leveling off and reaching a plateau and you decide the solution is to move it elsewhere as soon as possible. How do you evaluate your requirements? If you currently face some of the problems listed above, how can you be sure that you won't find similar difficulties in a new location? You can never be entirely sure until you have become

RATING WORKSHEET FOR A SMALL BUSINESS

If you are thinking of changing the location of all, or part, of your business, it will pay you to prepare some kind of worksheet which you can use to determine the best potential locations. The following is simply a guide, which you can adapt to your own use. Rate these features on a scale from one to ten — the higher the better.

OPERATIONS	RATING									
	1	2	3	4	5	6	7	8	9	10
Proximity to markets(s)										
Demographics of community										
Quality of life in area										
Employee availability										
Transportation										
Parking space										
Space for future expansion										
Traffic patterns										
Educational opportunities										
Location of competition										
Cost factors										
TOTAL RATINGS										

reestablished and are in business again, but, by taking the major factors into account as you analyze prospective new locations, you can virtually ensure that the move will achieve your goals.

Make sure of the following essential factors in your prospective location:

- A reliable market for your goods and services is available
- The local economy is stable
- Construction cost factors are within your range

- Maintenance for land and buildings is affordable
- Water supply is plentiful
- Power supply and other utilities are affordable
- Experienced personnel are at hand
- Transportation is adequate
- Taxes and assessments are manageable
- Business and commercial tax structures are supportive
- Quality of local services is high
- Fire protection is reliable
- Police protection and on-premises security are available

- Local ordinances and regulations are compatible
- Environmental quality is high and pollution is minimal
- Space is available for future expansion
- Residence facilities, such as schools, health and medical clinics, recreation, houses of worship, and stores are nearby
- The local government is stable and sound.

At the same time that you are investigating the positive factors, you should beware of circumstances that are potentially unfavorable for your business:

- A seasonal and fluctuating local economy
- Doubts about the steady demand for your goods or services
- Spreading pollution in the region
- Major controversies and political battles related to such topics as water supply, the ecology, highways, parking, taxation, and government.

Retail Location and Space Considerations

Although location is a factor in many types of business, this section will focus on retailing, because far and away the majority of small enterprises are retail stores. According to Irving Burstiner, author of *Run Your Own Store* and a consultant in the business field for more than 35 years, "these outlets are particularly vulnerable to failure due to the wrong location . . . . Success in a retail store depends to a large extent on the quantity and the quality of the traffic passing by. Most often, this is pedestrian traffic, though in some cases, the number of passing automobiles and available parking facilities can be of vital significance."

Factors in Choosing a Location

Among the key space factors for a growing retail business, he lists the following:

- Sufficient storage space for merchandise
- Work rooms and space for displays
- The extent of the store's **trading area,** which is the number of square miles it can service adequately
- The makeup of the local population
- The nature of the competition
- The compatibility of neighboring stores
- Parking facilities
- The availability of public transportation
- The volume of traffic
- The architecture and layout of the building
- The storefront.

Your volume of business now and in the future can be evaluated in direct relation to your location. Would you be better off on the other side of the street? On a more major street? On a side street? On a corner?

You should also consider whether your business would grow better in a different part of town. Here are the seven most common kinds of shopping and trading areas:

The "Main Street" location. This is the center of the business district, regardless of whether the geographic entity is a small town or a large city. You have to weigh the negative factors, like high rentals and maintenance costs against the positive factors, such as increased consumer traffic.

Neighborhood locations. These are areas where the population density is sufficient to support a substantial number of retail businesses. You can select a neighborhood that lacks much competition or is particularly compatible with your type of business (such as garden supplies and tools in a neighborhood where the homes have spacious plots and many eager amateur gardeners). But you have to do a higher per capita volume of business than you would in a heavily populated district.

General shopping centers. Situated on the outskirts of a city or town, these **shopping centers** practically guaranteeing heavy traffic in people who are specifically there to shop. This kind of location is advantageous if you can locate within your rental budget near the key consumer attraction, which may be a large department store, supermarket, or bank, rather than on the outskirts.

Regional malls. **Regional malls** often have a unifying motif and sometimes distinctive architecture, and which cater more to a neighborhood clientele than to city-wide consumers. Here, your advantages and disadvantages are similar to those in a small neighborhood shopping area.

Historic or theme malls. **Theme malls** may be located in one building (such as an abandoned and restored mill or old warehouse) or a group of interrelated buildings. This type of milieu is advantageous for high-price retail businesses or shops selling gifts, antiques, and other luxury items.

Affiliated business districts. Commercial centers located along major streets and highways leading into the heart of an urban area are known as **affiliated business districts.** These have the advantage of being major business districts with heavy traffic but with lower rents than the hub itself.

Interior Space Allocations

In the retailing business or, indeed, in any business where potential customers and clients come to your store or office, **store layout** is as important as geographical location when it comes to sales and marketing. The entrance(s) must be spacious and inviting and the space just inside must lead consumers steadily and persuasively toward other sections. The goal is to keep all areas as active and productive as possible.

You have probably already experimented with interior designs that serve this purpose, but it may be time to reevaluate your current setup. Here are some practical questions to ask about the layout and uses of your space:

- Is the space outside the building clean and inviting, particularly in the walks and approaches?
- Has enough space been allocated to the main entrance so it does not look cramped and claustrophobic?
- Is the space open enough so consumers coming through the entrance(s) can see several areas they may want to reconnoiter?
- If your business has more than one department — as in the case of a small department store, supermarket, or sporting goods shop — are divisions clearly and attractively marked?
- If the overall space occupies more than one floor or landing, do ramps, elevators, and stairs make it easy for people to move from one level to another?
- Has enough space been allocated to customer or patron service areas?

CHAPTER EIGHT

Recruiting and Reorienting Personnel for Growth

KEY TERMS FOR THIS CHAPTER

absenteeism

employee handbook

human resources planning (HRP)

morale

organizational chart

orientation

pay administration plan (PAP)

performance plan

turnover

As your small business grows and expands, you must give high priority to personnel management. While you are obviously concerned about such matters as the profit picture or plans for growth and expansion, realize that most small businesses succeed or fail on the basis of the *people* involved in their day-to-day functions. According to the National Personnel Association (NPA), one of the major factors in the success of small businesses is the ability of their owners and managers to recruit the right employees at the right time and for the right incentives and remuneration.

Many small companies have grown substantially because they have products that are in demand or because they address themselves to the needs that heretofore have not been fulfilled. Yet it has been well documented that these companies have also paid close attention to personnel needs and effective recruitment. In almost every case employee management has been well planned and implemented.

The ability of any small company to achieve its personnel goals depends to a large extent on the following factors:

- Sound management foresight and planning
- Availability of qualified workers and managers
- The precise and accurate communication of jobs specifications

JOB ANALYSIS CHECKLIST

One of the best ways to avoid personnel problems, such as absenteeism and low morale, is to make certain that all of the employees you hire have a clear image of the jobs they are to perform. The SBA suggests the following checklist as a starting point for evaluating each position as you wish to define it. (This may include redefining currently existing positions.) Add other items to the list in accordance with your own expectations.

Gather all data concerning the duties, qualifications, and responsibilities of the job:
- Consider these criteria and write them down clearly and in order of priority.
- Use a job analysis sheet to help you organize your thought and expectations for the assignment.
- Ask employees who now hold the same job, or parts of it, to list the duties responsibilities, and qualifications they believe are necessary for good performance.
- Review these essentials with the person who supervises the job, for similar input.

Keep in mind the ultimate goals of the analysis:
- To simplify employee recruitment
- To improve employee performance
- To prepare pertinent orientation and training to uphold the quality of performance
- To evaluate jobs so appropriate salaries and wage scales can be established.

- Fair and competitive salaries and wages at all levels, especially compared with other organizations in the same field
- Professional, dedicated personnel managers, whose fundamental responsibilities are directly related to employee recruitment or functions
- Effective training and orientation programs.

Modern personnel administration is divided into five segments, each of which is vital:

1. *Staffing,* to assure that managers with the proper skills and experience are assigned, even if only part time, to employee functions.

2. *Training and development,* with the goal of effectively utilizing employee capabilities and talents.

3. *Wage and salary administration,* properly researched and organized so the right people get sufficient remuneration in keeping with their contributions and loyalty to the business.

4. *Employee welfare,* which involves a considerable amount of research into available benefits and costs, and constant surveillance of support systems, legislation, and coordination.

5. *Record keeping,* a function that requires great accuracy and attention to detail in order to meet company and governmental specifications.

Planning Your Staff for Growth

Planned growth is far superior to the kind of expansion in which you just let things happen and then reorganize your operations and policies. And perhaps no other phase of planning is more vital than the steps you take to assure that you have the right people in the right places at the right times. As the head of one recruiting firm pointed out, it is more critical for a small company to plan accurately than it is for a large corporation because a small company does not have the financial reserves to rectify its mistakes. And, since you will be hiring comparatively few new staff members, you will both experience and cause a great deal of discomfort if, later, you have to let one or two of them go.

Major Features of Human Resources Planning

Human resources planning (HRP) is a responsibility of top management, whether in a small business like yours or in a large corporation. You should build into your plans and goals as soon as possible. It can help you to:

- Recruit employees
- Place people in the right positions
- Anticipate employment problems
- Consider employment solutions
- Motivate employees
- Lower the turnover rate

HRP is composed of the following sequential steps:

1. *The Inventory.* Take an inventory of your current employees, noting their specific job titles, salaries, qualifications, and relative experience. Where possible, note growth factors indicating which individuals have matured with the job and which have remained on plateaus.

2. *The Profile of Growth.* Pinpoint the changes in growth and development in your company that have taken place in the past, seem to be taking place today, and will probably take place in the future.

3. *Match People with Actions.* Show on paper as accurately as you can, which individuals have been matched with which fields of growth, and which are likely to match up with future patterns of changes.

4. *Turnover.* Chart the rate at which employee **turnover** has affected your business in the past and anticipate the turnover you expect in the future. Also, list a plan of action for lessening your turnover.

5. *Orientation.* Outline your plans for **orientation** and training — whether for new employees or for individuals moving from one position to another.

6. *Salary Administration.* A successful HRP needs a workable **pay administration plan (PAP).** This is a formal plan that lets employees know where they stand as far as salaries and bonuses and benefits are concerned. It also projects all major forms of recompense into the future, thus alerting employees to future opportunities and their chances of raises and promotions.

Employee Growth Plan

Having taken stock of the current situation, you are ready to enact your employee growth plan, starting with the managers and supervisors and then following up with lower-level employees. Your employee growth plan should include the following four steps:

1. Determine which departments or operations are growing the fastest, then list your personnel needs for supervisors, specialists, and others, and set a deadline for hiring them.

2. Define the requirements and qualifications for each position you will fill. Categorize them into groups, if appropriate, in particular areas of activity.

3. Prepare a schedule for successive steps in implementing the personnel plan, such as (a)

JOB ORIENTATION CHECKLIST

The following are suggestions and thought-stimulators to help you determine what points should be covered when interviewing or introducing a new employee to the company:

- Company's status
- Company's goals
- Description of job
- Related jobs
- Tie-ins, if any, to those jobs
- Explanation of pertinent facilities
- Areas in building to tour with new employee
     - Headquarters Office
     - Plant
     - Laboratory
     - Cafeteria
     - Computer facilities
     - Transportation area
     - Employee Facilities
     - Accounting and business department
     - Other
- Review of duties and responsibilities
- Review of compensation and benefits
- Introduction to other employees
- Questions and answers

---

searching, (b) contacting, (c) interviewing, (d) deciding, and (e) hiring.

4. Prepare a communications plan, so everyone concerned — whether old hands or newcomers — will be aware of your reasoning and supportive of personnel growth and development.

The Road to More Rewarding Recruitment

Employees have been described as the mother lode that determines whether a company is hitting pay dirt or just plain grubbing to stay solvent. Too many managers, especially those in small businesses, look upon recruitment as a kind of seasonal phenomenon they have to put up with. They try to anticipate when the market is going to be down and times are tough enough so they can find willing workers at lower pay scales with little more effort than placing a few want ads in the local papers. This approach is a sure way to slow your future pattern of growth.

You cannot expect to recruit the best people unless you assign this function top priority and administer it yourself or through an able and dedicated personnel director. Never look down at jobs that do not require a high level of education. Recruiting people with sound educational backgrounds and mental capacities will energize your company's creative activities in every field, from research, marketing, and sales to production, management, and transportation. One entrepreneur asserts that small-business owners and personnel directors should "hire the person, not the position." He claims that people who have heart are more valuable in the long run than those who call themselves experts.

He adds another valuable point: Always hire people you respect. Employees are quick to perceive management attitudes and will react to such opinions with a corresponding positive or negative manner.

Staffing Tips

It is well worth reviewing the following points made by Richard Gallagher in *Your Small Business Made Simple* and applying them to your personnel needs as your company continues to grow.

- Hire key people yourself when you can do so without interrupting other higher-priority duties, but learn how to judge the reliability of professional employment agencies and apprise them of your needs where possible.
- Never assume that employees will have a clear understanding of their responsibilities; make these duties crystal clear at the outset.
- As your organization becomes larger, study its departmental structure and make sure it is serving effectively.
- Review your **organizational chart** periodically. This chart shows the relationship of all positions and departments within your business, and it will help you to determine how well your key employees are aligned to perform their jobs.
- Promptly remedy any situation in which subordinates receive conflicting instructions from their supervisors, and examine the unity of command.

- Make realistic plans for a successor, whether temporary or permanent, in the event that you should become disabled.

Reorientation: Training Your Employees for Growth

Companies that grow have histories of continuing evaluation and reorientation. Their managers keep abreast of the times, insist that their associates do so as well, and provide their employees with practical, relevant, and easily accessible training programs geared to changing needs and objectives.

According to the American Management Association, one of the common shortcomings among owners and managers of small businesses is to "expect supervisors and employees to have the same intensity, learning skills, and commitments" as the people who run the company. It is taken for granted that employees who are technicians, specialists, or otherwise experienced are hired because they have the necessary skills and capabilities. Yet, even when they are highly skilled, they may not know how to use their talents to full advantage within the company unless they receive basic orientation about their jobs and goals, and unless they receive the training to perform their work properly and efficiently.

When a company grows, it is vital for its people at all levels, from top management on down, to reorient themselves, sometimes dramatically. The company that has eighty-four employees is no longer what it was with eighteen employees. The retail store that does $4 million worth of business annually is no longer the little emporium that grossed $200,000 in sales. The service that has 160 clients barely resembles the business that had forty-six patrons. Newly hired managers and employees are sometimes more qualified than those who have been with the organization since the start because they have a different, more accurate perspective of the current situation and economic conditions.

Planned orientation is a vital, ongoing activity that requires your attention. Proper training can anticipate and eliminate many job-related headaches. How do you plan and activate this kind of orientation? You can do it yourself — if you are qualified and understand the educational process and its many ramifications. But the chances are that you will be much better off if you call in an educational consultant for advice, preferably a specialist who has worked extensively with small businesses. A consultant can help you establish clear objectives, set up training procedures and schedules, and motivate employees to participate, for the mutual benefit of the employee and the company.

A few of the advantages that accrue from continuing orientation and training:

- Improved management
- More effective supervision
- Closer communication at all levels
- Increased business
- Continuing growth and expansion
- Better employee **morale**
- Lower turnover rate
- Less waste
- Increased productivity
- Reduced operational costs
- More effective technical development.

Effective Training = Good Performance

"Think of the last time you attempted a task for which you lacked the necessary skill — cooking a meal if you are not a cook . . . struggling through a computer system you have never used before, or trying to figure out how a new phone system works . . ." Management consultants Garry Jacobs and Robert MacFarlane ask clients to recall how they felt when trying to cope with situations with which they were unfamiliar and for which they had never been trained.

Do you remember similar experiences? Have you also had the opposite experience when you taught yourself a new skill or a way to perform a formerly unfamiliar function, and were able to accomplish it? Learning how to transform the unfamiliar into the familiar can be a satisfying and exciting experience. Bear this in mind when you plan informal orientation programs or more formal training sessions to help your employees perform better.

You should be able to rough out a chart or outline showing which functions and operations seem to be flowing most smoothly from the personnel standpoint, and which have rough spots that obstruct your goals and expectations. How many employees in these work areas seem to need more orientation and education? How many are functioning smoothly and might even serve as instructors to assist their fellow employees in upgrading performance?

The Performance Plan

Training and performance go hand in hand. As you plan your orientation programs, make sure that all managers and the people who report to them are aware of performance goals. Your **performance plan** should include the following steps to motivate employees to attain those goals:

- Set wage and salary scales that are perceived by employees as fair compensation for their work.
- Initiate equity or profit-sharing plans to give employees a share in the business, even if modest.
- Introduce programs regarding safety, ethics, cleanliness, neatness, and appearance so that employees take pride in their work and surroundings.
- Give proper recognition to accomplishments in such a way that they will inspire other employees.
- Define the avenues employees can take to achieve promotions, earn raises, and otherwise profit from better job performance.
- Communicate your short-term and long-range goals, as well as more immediate objectives, so employees can see the big picture.
- Insofar as possible, recruit people who not only are qualified for the jobs but who evidence high levels of enthusiasm, vigor, and health.

Positive Personnel Management

Some small businesses are much more vulnerable than others to problems that affect personnel management. Department stores, for example, are noted for an excessive number of impolite, indifferent, or uninformed employees. Many of the causes are frustrating and almost beyond control, such as the seasonal nature of selling and marketing, low pay, sparse benefits, and limited chances for job advancement.

However, a study of retail marketing by the Small Business Administration brought out factors of positive management — the kind of actions that lessened, if they did not actually solve, some of the chronic problems faced by small-business owners:

- Creating communication with the public and with employment agencies to announce expected openings well in advance
- Offering more bonuses and discounts for employees, based on length of service
- Giving awards to recognize effective on-the-job performance
- Organizing of employee social events
- Improving the company image and, by extension, the status of people who are associated with it
- Providing car pools, vans, and other forms of transportation to make commuting more comfortable
- Hiring more people who are disabled yet able to exercise above-average efficiency when placed in the right jobs
- Continuing dialogue between top management and the rank and file employees.

Suggestions for Handling People

If you want to know more about communicating effectively with employees and motivating them to support your business objectives, take a tip from Gene Garofalo, a marketing and sales manager with long experience in dealing with company personnel. He recommends the following steps to assure employee cooperation and interest:

- Create dialogues and respect opinions that differ from yours.
- Underreact rather than overreact to avoid escalating a tense or sensitive situation, or hindering the dialogue.
- Before facing a difficult discussion with an employee, rehearse what you want to say.
- When speaking with staff members about a touchy subject, use the "feel-felt-found" ap-

proach: "I know how you *feel*" . . . "I have *felt* that way myself" . . . "In the end, I *found* that . . ."

- Never patronize or act in a condescending manner to employees.
- Be assertive. State your views and directions in a firm, but non-aggressive, manner.
- Be precise. When an action must be taken, explain it in no uncertain terms.
- Be complimentary in a forthright way and praise staff members and employees who deserve commendation.
- Be sincere, and do not flatter an employee when praise is not deserved.
- Avoid debate. It is important to listen to employee viewpoints, but don't use a disagreement as an excuse to test your verbal skills.
- Be positive when announcing new policies, programs, and restrictions, without reference to disagreements that may have preceded the final decision.

How to Be a Better Manager

An editorial in *Personnel Journal*, whose readers are actively involved with human resources in companies large and small, stated that many business experts consider people to be a company's most vital resource. Since in most instances labor is the greatest financial outlay to which a company is committed, it seems logical that this area should be managed with efficiency and dedication. It is important for you and your human resources supervisors to evaluate personnel requirements on a regular basis, and especially during any period when the company is undergoing changes that affect employees directly. If too many people are employed and some are sitting idle, the company is flushing profits down the drain. However, when there are not enough employees to han-

dle the work load, the situation is equally devastating, and can have a number of negative consequences, including:

- Dissatisfaction of employees who feel they are being used by the company
- Accidents as a result of failures by overworked supervisors to detect risky work practices
- Damage to products being produced or assembled because employees are tired or rushed
- Poor public relations and a decrease in job applications from the outside.

Companies that face seasonal changes or marked fluctuations in input and output for any reason are particularly vulnerable to the problem of too many or too few people. They, above all, need expert personnel supervisors and management planners who can alleviate these difficulties. An experienced personnel manager, for example, can achieve flexibility by determining when it is most feasible to have available a cadre of part-time workers. Yet it is a tricky, often sensitive situation. Employees may not like to be labeled "part-timers," and may feel (often justifiably) that they are second-class citizens who are treated unfairly in such matters as benefits, vacation time, and remuneration.

Another problem that surfaces frequently and requires the attention of a real pro is the matter of layoffs and cut-backs. More often than not, the company, rather than the employee, is at fault. The company may be caught in a bind because of severe business losses, a dip in the economy, or inroads made by an aggressive competitor. In such situations, when employees whose work has been satisfactory have to be let go, a sensitive personnel supervisor can trim the ranks without kindling rancor, animosity, or legal repercussions.

REDUCING THEFT AND LOSS

As business grows, there is often an increase in vulnerability to criminal activity in the form of petty theft, grand larceny, embezzlement, shoplifting, employee pilferage, or record falsifications, as well as the more violent crimes of robbery and burglary. Consider the following ways to detect and prevent such loss.

• Notify employees that "snitching" small, inexpensive items like office pencils and pens has to be curtailed and often leads to larger and larger thefts.

• Assign two people with non-monetary duties to check any functions that relate to the handling of money and other valuables.

• Establish procedures to follow in the event employees are faced with burglary or break-ins.

• Train employees to be alert, and to keep an eye on strangers who might be in a position to remove valuables in an office, workshop, or other location.

• Establish a system that offers access to offices and work areas only by way of entrances that are properly staffed and supervised.

• Hire people whose past employment records can be checked and make it known from the beginning that honesty and trust are vital in your organization.

• Maintain accurate, tamperproof financial records in accordance with acceptable accounting procedures.

• Establish effective supervision in all areas related to shipping and receiving operations.

• Ascertain that all cash disbursements have the approval of a trusted supervisor.

• Maintain close control over the issuance and storage of keys, and allow keys to be checked out only to personnel who need them for specific duties.

• Install effective security and alarm systems on all premises.

• Purchase high-quality safes and other containers for valuables that have been documented as tamperproof and fireproof.

• Provide adequate illumination for interior and exterior locations that could be subject to breaking and entering.

Dealing with Other Personnel Problems

You should never try to lump people problems in one category, since there are far too many variables and circumstances. One employee might not be working effectively because of an illness in the family, while another may not be motivated by the task at hand. But one recurring problem facing most businesses is **absenteeism.** A business that has been established for some time will reveal a certain pattern of absenteeism, depending upon the nature of the work and the kinds of fluctuation that accompany it. Companies that, for example, often require employees to work outdoors in inclement weather are likely to have a larger percentage of absences than those whose employees work comfortably indoors. The no-shows may use colds and other aches and pains as excuses. Periods of stress often result in an increased degree of absenteeism. Certain periods of the

WHAT KIND OF AN EMPLOYEE GUIDE OR HANDBOOK DO I NEED?

Your employees and the company alike would benefit from a publication — not too complicated, and yet not too sparse — that provides guidelines relating to jobs, benefits, goals, the
organization's background and history, policies, the community personnel services, and the
like. Here's an alphabetical list of some points to cover in your **employee handbook,** as recommended by the Small Business Administration:

Absence from work	Parking and transportation
Benefits	Past and present growth
Bonuses	Pay periods
Coffee breaks	Profit sharing
Community benefits	Publications
Company policies	Recreational periods
Complaints	Rest facilities
Education and training	Retirement
Equal employment opportunities	Social Security
Future plans for expansion	Sports programs
Goals and objectives	Substance abuse
Health and fitness programs	Telephone usage
History and background	Unemployment compensation
Holidays	Vacations
Insurance	Work facilities
Meals, snacks, and beverages	Working hours
Medical assistance	Other subjects to cover: _____
Military leave	_____
Old-age benefits	_____

year also generate absenteeism, and the "Mon-
day syndrome" — higher absenteeism after the
weekend — is commonplace, as is absence on
the days following holidays.

Controlling absenteeism is a management
function that often needs attention and tight-
ening, since it can contribute to profits and
growth when effectively administered. One
company that paid weekly wages cut absenteeism in half by distributing paychecks on Mon-
days instead of Fridays. A guidebook on
absenteeism (Management Aid #206), published by the Small Business Administration,
describes a successful experiment in which the
owner of a small company eliminated vacations
and sick leave. In their place, he gave each
employee 30 days annual leave to use as the
employee saw fit. At the end of the year, his
workers were paid for any of the 30 days they
had not used. "As a result," reported the SBA,
"unscheduled absences and overtime pay were
reduced significantly. In addition, employees
were happier and more productive than they
were under the old system."

Internal Communications

Now that you've evaluated the ways in which your enterprise is growing and planned for its more effective management, you must now stay on top of the basic functions and operations that are the lifeblood of your company. These include communications, marketing, financial accounting, advertising and promotion, record keeping, and the other basics of sound administration.

The major artery running through your company is communication. The objectives of **internal communication** in a growing business include:

- Presenting information about new developments in the firm
- Explaining the unfamiliar, such as state-of-the-art technologies, recent acquisitions, improved equipment, or newly created positions and duties
- Clarifying policies
- Reasserting current policies in the face of related changes

- Eliminating surprises and unexpected situations as transitions occur
- Boosting morale, especially at times when there are positive factors that rank and file employees may not be aware of
- Clearing up differences between managers or partners
- Soliciting **feedback.**

Coordination and Cooperation

When a company has been having problems with the **coordination** of its functions or obtaining the required **cooperation** of its employees, the cause is usually poor communication. One major company found a successful solution by installing small television receivers in its various departments and its cafeteria and transmitting information telecasts, which the

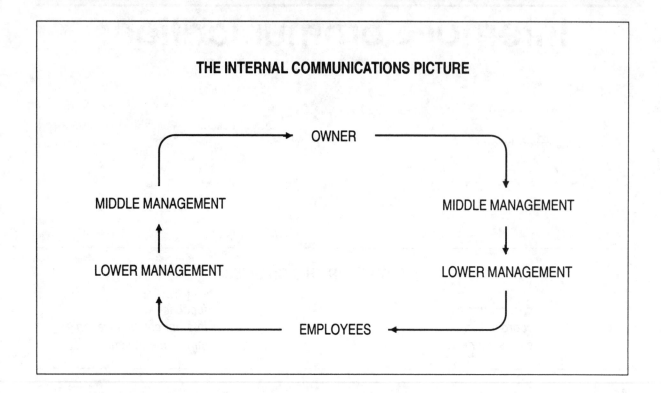

THE INTERNAL COMMUNICATIONS PICTURE

employees could receive at the push of a button. These provided news about products and services, benefits, recreational programs, and technological advances in the industry, in segments ranging from five minutes to an hour's duration.

Your firm may be too small for anything this elaborate, but you can still communicate effectively through newsletters, bulletin-board displays, posters, or short group briefings on pertinent topics.

Consider taking occasional **employee surveys** to determine how your workers feel about company policies, operations, benefits, services, or other matters of direct concern to them. Such surveys should also provide an opportunity to solicit productive suggestions. Giving employees a voice has proved to be a morale booster for many companies, and has often been instrumental in lowering absenteeism, preventing accidents, and improving job satisfaction.

Whatever the medium selected when communicating with your employees, maintain a positive, constructive tone. If you feel the necessity to explain certain policies or actions, do so in an enthusiastic way. Make no excuses, and never get into a bind by saying (or implying) "We don't really want to do such and such, but we are forced into it because . . . ."

The Value of Listening

Communicating is a two-way street. Say all you want to, but never forget that you also have to listen. One successful manager referred to this process as the **mirror phenomenon.** You beam your message in the direction of your employees, but then you also encourage them to reflect their impressions and beliefs back to you. This is critical in the case of employees whom you do not see very often, such as sales people who are constantly on the road, or workers whose assignments are far from headquarters. Here are some tips for improving the listening/communicating relationship:

1. Communicate information to employees by whatever method is likely to be most effective within a given budget.

2. Make it easy for employees to give verbal or written playbacks.

3. Make it clear that you are listening and welcome opinions and suggestions.

4. Follow up any playback by acknowledging that you have received it and gotten the message.

5. Act promptly on all matters that require follow-through or acknowledgement.

One of the benefits of active internal communication, with an emphasis on listening, is that employees who have to deal with customers, clients, suppliers, or other outsiders will in turn communicate much more articulately and productively. Responsiveness and dialogue lead to such benefits as improved sales, a better company image, new customers, better relations with financial institutions, and easier recruiting. The feedback you get depends upon the quality and the frequency of your communications.

The Language of Communications

Many owners and managers of small businesses complain that they are, as one expressed it, "very frustrated because we try to communicate all the time to our employees and listen to their gripes and desires, but we seem to get very little response."

The problem is often one of language. You must write or speak in terms that can be clearly understood by everyone for whom the message is intended. Train yourself to think in terms of the audience to whom you are speaking or writing, whether it's one person or several hundred. Are these people familiar with technical terminology? With company and industry issues? With specialized words and phrases used by supervisors, executives, and the business office?

When you find that you do have to use terms that might not be familiar, don't hesitate to explain or define them. You can do so in a forthright manner, without talking down to the reader or listener. Here are some typical examples:

• "Your company has decided to expand into the field of *cryogenics*. This is the science related to extreme cold and thus would be a natural for us, since we already manufacture parts for refrigerators and freezers."

• "It has been suggested that we enlarge our company fitness program by adding sessions on *aerobics*, which have to do with strengthening the heart and lungs through exercises like jogging, cycling, and swimming."

• "We have been asked by the county prosecutor's office to warn our employees that many people in our community are being victimized by *boiler room schemes*. This is the type of scam in which you receive a phone call urging you to send money right away to the caller's firm and buy into very cheap stocks that are going to multiply quickly in value."

• "The *stock option plan* we are offering employees who have been with us for a year or more can best be defined as an opportunity for you to buy stock in the company at a discount price and thus, in effect, become a part owner of the business."

Many companies that are steadily growing are in this enviable position because they are venturing into new fields or acquiring related businesses in order to broaden their potential for the future. When such events happen, it is

COMMUNICATIONS FLOW CHART

Below is a checklist of internal channels of communication, recipients of information, and frequency of contacts.

MEDIUM OF COMMUNICATION	AUDIENCES REACHED	FREQUENCY
Memos		
Letters		
Newsletters		
Telephone		
Fax		
Clippings		
Reports		
Company publications		
Internal video system		
Personal visits		
Other media		

not only beneficial, but almost mandatory, to inform managers, supervisors, and other key personnel about the nature of these new enterprises and functions. When communicating such information, be as brief and concise as possible, yet be sure to include descriptions, definitions, and in some cases even specifications that will clarify the subject.

If the new venture is substantially different from your existing field(s) of operation, your best recourse might be to attach or include a printed piece that is informative, yet not too formidable in format and detail. A practical example is that of the owner of a small plant engaged in the manufacture of shoes. To reduce his production costs, he decided to purchase one of his suppliers, another small manufacturer, which specialized in dyes formulated for leather goods. Since he wanted to modify some of these dyes for the retail market,

he had to communicate the appropriate information to his marketing personnel. He did this by taking the highly technical data specification sheets written by the firm's chemists, had them translated into a consumer leaflet, and distributed this, with a covering memo, to all of his sales people.

In this manner, he communicated effectively, both internally and externally, and converted unfamiliar subject matter into everyday language.

Encourage Questions and Responsiveness

An essential part of good internal communications is an atmosphere in which people are not only readily able to ask questions and respond, but actively encouraged to do so. Curiosity and the determination to become knowledgeable are prime nourishment for growth, both for individuals and the companies for which they work. Here are seven key recommendations to convey to your employees, at all levels from management to mailroom:

1. When you receive instructions from your boss, or any manager or supervisor, be sure you understand them thoroughly before you act.

2. If the meaning of such instructions is foggy in your mind, ask for clarification. Don't be afraid to take up someone's time to get the facts straight.

3. Establish your own communications system — perhaps a report or regular memo — to help your superiors keep abreast of current progress. This provides a constructive opportunity for them to revise your course of action if they see a way to improve it.

4. If for any reason you anticipate a delay in fulfilling an assignment, report this promptly, instead of at the last minute. If the project needs some form of assistance to meet the original deadline, make productive suggestions or requests.

5. State your objections tactfully, but firmly, if you feel that job instructions are off course or your skills and experience are not being put to good use.

6. Take whatever steps are necessary to understand the reasons that have motivated instructions regarding your work. When you know why you have been assigned a certain job, you will be in a better position to fulfill it or suggest revisions.

7. Avoid the habit of questioning instructions unless you have serious misgivings about the judgment behind them.

PART THREE

MARKETING

CHAPTER TEN

Salesmanship in Transition

KEY TERMS FOR THIS CHAPTER

consumer trends	*management style*
cycles	*sales curve*
leadership	*sales management*

The more your business expands, the more important the selling function becomes. We think of selling in terms of moving products, marketing materials, or promoting the use of services. Yet the continuing growth of your company mandates that you also take steps to sell such intangibles as your company's name and image, and to improve the public's impression of your industry. This overall public image is part of the environment in which your business's sales are likely to flourish.

The Management of Sales Markets

The growth of a company that sells goods and services is dependent to a large extent on the ability of the owner(s) to anticipate changes in market conditions and consumer preferences. While it is possible to create new markets and change **consumer trends** and tastes, these functions are more likely to be motivated by large corporations, which have substantial advertising and public relations budgets, than by small businesses where money is tight.

You should be constantly alert to commercial and consumer trends that might lead to healthy sales when properly exploited, or to a downtrend for you if ignored. When you foresee pockets of stagnation, don't try to bully your way through them. Instead, look for pockets of opportunity, which may require the marketing of somewhat different products or modifications in the kinds of service you offer. Stick-to-it-iveness may be a commendable quality for certain pursuits in life. But in sales, stubbornness and the determination to push products, goods, and services down consumers' throats can only lead to red ink on your ledger.

When a small firm named Computer Keys, Ltd., opened its doors in a small town in the environs of Columbia, South Carolina, it thrived on business from the nearby state capital, where there were many offices engaged in work requiring data-processing assistance. But the work load tapered off as more and more clients established their own internal computer networks. At first, CK's three partners attempted to regain business through more aggressive advertising, attendance at corporate conferences, and direct-mail solicitation. Nothing worked — not until Abe Treadway, one of the partners, read an article in *Business Week* about the disturbing increase in "viruses," programs deliberately created and injected into computer systems to disrupt them. At his suggestion, the company changed its name to Keyboard Solutions and circulated the word through press releases and media contacts that it was specializing in consultation and programming to help clients fight these invasions and protect their computer data banks. Business quickly improved for the company because very few firms in the area were knowledgeable about this new threat to their computer facilities and were not trained or equipped to avoid serious disruptions.

How to Keep Abreast of Trends that Affect Your Business

When evaluating current and future sales predictions, ask yourself these questions:

• What products and/or services that we have to offer will remain level?

• Which have peaked and are likely to decline in demand?

• Which are likely to increase in demand?

• What changes or additions can we make to our current line of products to bring about an upward **sales curve?**

• How can we modify or expand the services we offer to make them more attractive in the short and long-term?

• Should we sell or phase out any part of our present business and invest the income or savings in a new venture with more potential for the future?

• How do we think our immediate competitors are faring in regard to the above questions?

The Management of Goods and Services

Once you have established a clear overview of current and future markets, your next step should be to zero in on the specifics of what you have to offer. Obviously, those products and services that promise the greatest potential for sales and profits should rate higher priorities than those than are questionable or downright losers. As a starter, take a piece of paper and jot down the potential of each item or group of items you are offering the public. Break them into operational categories, such as consumer products, technical or specialized products, materials, resources, personnel, consultation, services, and the like. Then rate each of them on the basis of one (the lowest) to ten (the highest) in regard to marketability and contribution to profits.

The next step is to double-check with partners, staff members, or others who can verify your opinions or suggest revisions. With this information on hand, consider which items to drop entirely, which to replace, which to put on hold for the time being, and which to promote aggressively on the market. Bear in mind that many products and services run through **cycles** as follows:

OPERATIONAL LIFE CYCLES THAT AFFECT YOUR BUSINESS

To obtain a clearer picture of which products and services are most subject to peaks and cycles, list at the left the products and/or services you supply to your customers or clients. Under "Cycles" note whether the trend is up, down, or steady. How often during the year? And in which seasonal periods?

If a product or service commonly goes through more than one cycle a year, list that item on two or more lines.

With this information before you, determine what steps you can take to eliminate or improve these cycles.

	CYCLES				
PRODUCTS AND SERVICES	RISE	FALL	STEADY	FREQUENCY	DATES
Products:					
Services:					

- A steady rise in demand, reaching a peak, and then declining to point zero (such as this year's calendar)
- Fluctuating demands, rising and falling with seasonal periods (such as winter coats or swimsuits)
- Level demands, with little fluctuation (such as food staples)
- Intermittent demands (such as recordings that may be very popular, then die out and become fads many years later).

Since you have been in business for some time, you probably already have a handle on these cycles and where your own goods and services fit in. But it is well worth the time and effort to put your thoughts and experience on paper and get the objective opinions of your colleagues.

Need a New Market? Look for the Commonplace!

When entrepreneurs look for ways to boost business, they too often try to be ingenious and, as a result, overlook common markets that are practically staring them in the face. Paul Hawken, a highly successful entrepreneur who founded Erewhon, the largest distributor of natural foods, and Smith & Hawken, the premier mail-order garden tool company, advises other entrepreneurs, "Take a prosaic, everyday, kick-around sort of product and make it real again. Hamburgers, for example. There are so many bad hamburgers in this world I venture to say anyone with a hot grill who makes an honest one with generous portions and fresh onions will never lack for customers. In other words, take a product and reduce it to its essence."

He recalled how he once was hired by a fuel company, as a consultant, to develop a market for its charcoal, which was made from mesquite logs. "But mesquite is more than a fuel," he explained. "It burns at 1,700 degrees, instead of the 700 degrees generated by standard charcoal briquets, and sears meat quickly, locking in flavor as well as adding its own unique flavor." He suggested that his client differentiate his supposedly commonplace product from the really commonplace by changing the briquette-style packaging and selling mesquite as an ingredient and not just a fuel. As Hawken stated with justifiable pride, "Business soared."

He pointed also to the way in which Korean immigrants preempted the fresh produce-market business in New York City by taking very commonplace products, displaying them in a way that made vegetables and fruit look fresh and appetizing, and at the same time maintaining competitive prices. Other similar examples are those of a handful of entrepreneurs who realized that, while supermarkets stocked endless supplies of cookies, there was seldom a really yummy-looking cookie in sight. They took advantage of the situation and transformed a commonplace item into a luxury-priced best-seller by dressing it up and displaying it in mouthwatering glory.

Think of ways in which you, too, might provide the magic touch for your products or services that would brighten your sales picture, even during a downtrend.

Sales Management and Leadership

Whether you are serving as your business's sales director or whether you have turned the responsibility over to another manager, here are six keys to continued growth in sales. These **sales management** tips are supplied courtesy of the Small Business Administration:

1. *Think like a manager.* Maintain your position as the top executive, yet at the same time delegate authority in such a way that salespeople are working hard for you, not standing on the sidelines and watching you perform.

2. *Respect time.* Learn how to plan your hours and days so you allocate the right level of priority and time to the sales and marketing projects in which you need to be involved.

3. *Work with people more than things.* The primary rule of good sales management is to spend at least three-quarters of your time working with people and one-quarter or less on administrative details, most of which can be effectively delegated.

THE QUALITIES OF LEADERSHIP

A successful British sales executive, Gordon Selfridge, has noted the differel bosses and leaders:

Bosses . . .	Leaders . . .
Shout orders	Provide guidance
Drive their employees	Orient their employees
Depend on authority	Succeed through good will
Arouse fear	Stimulate enthusiasm
Speak about "I"	Refer mostly to "We"
Fix blame for breakdowns	Fix the breakdowns
Order people to "Go!"	Say "Let's go!" to all

4. *Develop a management style.* You will be a better manager if you can develop a **management style** that is fitting to your personality and ties in with your objectives. You don't have to be a showman, but a steady and recognizable way of acting and relating to your salespeople will make it easier for them to know what to expect from you.

5. *Know your sales personnel.* You should not only know all of the people under your jurisdiction, but you should also maintain at least an informal checklist of their qualifications, experience, character traits, and even their shortcomings. This kind of ready knowledge makes it easier to assign the right people to the right job and plan training programs for those who need more orientation.

6. *Act like a leader.* Too few owners and mangers of small businesses are true leaders who can count on having people follow them because they exert proper guidance. **Leadership** is, of course, a complex attribute that is difficult to define, but the methods by which leaders operate can be pinpointed. Here are some of the ways sales managers develop effective leadership and motivate their salespeople:

• They develop a vigorous style, which their people strive to emulate as they present themselves to others and deal with prospective customers, clients, and patrons.

• They actively encourage their salespeople when things look good and reassure them that the picture will change when things look bad.

• They set examples through hard work, devotion to the company, responsiveness, and determination to be the best in the business.

• They motivate others to produce by setting realistic goals, grooming people for promotion, and providing bonuses and other meaningful rewards.

• They publicize newsworthy information about successful sales, sales records, promotions, and significant personal accomplishments, both on the job and off.

• They "turn the other cheek" when sales slump, avoiding excuses and reprimands and predicting strong upturns in the near future.

SALES TRAINING CHECKLIST

To determine how well you are managing salespeople, use this form or the equivalent to initiate and maintain sales training checklists for everyone working in your business on a full- or part-time basis. Select actual accounts that are being solicited. The ratings of "good," "fair," or "poor" can come from five sources:

1. Your own familiarity with the person and the account.
2. Impressions and opinions from supervisors and managers on the accounts in question.
3. Person-to-person interviews with the salesperson involved.
4. The salesperson's written report.
5. The customer, when you are in a position to discuss the account tactfully.

Name of Business Account			
Description			
Sales Person Assigned			
ACTIVITY	GOOD	FAIR	POOR
Advance preparation			
Knowledge of product or service			
Homework for customer's business			
Homework for contact			
Introductory approach			
Presentation			
Questions and answers			
Objections overcome			
Materials used			
Closing			
Follow-through			
Future action planning			

THE Q&A FORMAT

Sales training (or any other kind of training) need not be lengthy and complicated. One of the best methods is the Question & Answer approach. In this case, however, you are not asking the questions but training your salespeople in Q&A skills. The following are some typical questions for them to ask themselves before approaching prospects:

- What specific products and/or services am I going to try to sell today?
- How much do I know about the person(s) I will be contacting?
- Do I know what my customer's interests are and what topics are likely to spark the most favorable reaction?
- If this is a new prospect, where has he or she been turning for the products and/or services I hope to sell?
- Have I anticipated any objections or other negatives that are likely to kill the sale, and have I decided on a positive response?
- What do I plan in the way of follow-up?

A good question to ask yourself: Are you worried that too much training will bore your employees to tears? Don't be. A top-ranking sales manager asserts very decisively: "There are two nevers to remember about sales training. The first is that sales people can never be overtrained. The second is that sales training never ends."

- They teach and inform continuously, whether through casual discussions about new products and markets or in formalized seminars and orientation programs.

Educating Your Sales Force

As one successful sales manager expressed it, "Sales training is like feeding your children healthy, well-balanced diets. It's tough to say anything against it."

But management in a growing company does have to do its homework and decide just what is healthy and well balanced when it comes to establishing training programs. There are eight reasons why continuous sales orientation is necessary, whether it is in the nature of informal meetings or well-structured seminars:

1. In our increasingly technological culture, procedures, equipment, and materials change rapidly.

2. Competition gets keener in those areas of small business that have proven successful, and the survivors are likely to be those that are well educated.

3. Training programs at all levels represent a logical and credible way of communicating company policies and objectives, as well as sales facts, without seeming to preach.

4. Because the costs for maintaining a sales force are constantly climbing, it is essential to receive useful playback from every sales call.

5. A well-prepared and well-directed training program will inspire and motivate your salespeople. Frequency and regularity of training are very important.

6. Well-trained salespeople reflect not only knowledge of their field but the kind of professionalism that gives customers confidence in their products and services.

7. Customers tend to buy from salespeople who are able to demonstrate the use of products clearly or who can document services in a convincing way.

8. Well-trained salespeople are able to field almost any question thrown at them, making them more effective, more enthusiastic, and more comfortable in their jobs.

Growing Public Relations

Public relations is a positive form of communication that can enhance your business image in the community. It can be quite simple and direct in the case of a small firm or very complex as employed by a large corporation. You can use public relations to your advantage, even if you have only on or two staff members assigned to the job on a part-time basis. Public relations will help your organization to grow by maintaining its momentum when things are going smoothly, bridging the gaps when the going gets rough, and highlighting those areas that promise a vigorous, rewarding future.

As Richard Gallagher wrote in *Your Small Business Made Simple*, "Public relations is more subtle than publicity. Public relations campaigns are designed to make people think well of a business . . . . Good public relations is more than a series of strategies; it is an attitude of wanting to put something back into the community in return for what you receive from it. Good **public relations** is treating all customers courteously. It is keeping your premises tidy and in good repair. It is pulling the weeds around street trees when the city does not get to it."

The ABCs of Public Relations

Public relations today is more than a series of **press releases** or an information service for people who write or phone the company. A comprehensive public relations plan for your business should encompass your company's image in the community, its relations and communications with the outside world, and internal relations as well. The kind of P.R. you are most likely to find useful will include some or all of the following:

- Determining the nature and extent of the significant **public** you want to reach, both internal (such as employees and stockholders) and external (such as customers, suppliers, government officials, and the **media**)
- Defining the **image** the company most wants to project to the public
- Upgrading communications equipment, such as computers, word processors, picturephones, photocopying machines, audio and video devices, and fax equipment
- Developing state-of-the-art methods for transmitting information, whether by ordinary mail, express mail, electronics, or even by hand
- Building reliable contacts with professionals in radio, television, newspapers, magazines, and other media
- Preparing news releases, fact sheets, graphics, and business reports of many kinds
- Preparing procedures and methods for providing factual information promptly in times of crisis
- Learning how to hold **press conferences**
- Improving relationships with clients and/or customers
- Establishing plans for maintaining and improving **employee relations**
- Training managers and supervisors in the art of being positive spokespersons for the company and industry
- Working with an outside P.R. firm or a professional consultant
- Public speaking on behalf of an organization or on issues favorable to your business
- Investigating the value of **archives,** records of your company's history, even for relatively young businesses, in promoting favorable patterns and notable achievements of the past
- Establishing **codes of ethics,** mainly for internal use, but on occasion communicating them externally to customers, suppliers, and the general public
- Planning and promoting programs that help keep your operations compatible with the environment and making sure the public thinks of your company as ecologically sound
- Convincing people, internally and externally, that your organization's historical values are in keeping with the heritage of the community
- Improving your organization's selection and use of names and slogans for products, processes, services, and programs so they are contemporary and not offensive to any group
- Organizing **special events** that help sell the company.

Special Events that Help Sell the Company

As small businesses grow older, their owners and managers become increasingly aware of activities and programs that are of interest to their community — whether they are related to history, recreation, food, sports, music, drama, or nature. It makes sense from a public relations viewpoint for businesses large and small to take advantage of programs they can initiate, or at least participate in. When a company is associated with something from which the public derives pleasure, education, or pride, that company is likely to attract more business.

Following a Founder's Day program that was created, organized, and largely sponsored by a local lumber works, the mayor of a small town in New England said, "How can you not feel a glow of appreciation for the firm that erected ingenious props on the village green, using its own products and craftsmen? And why would you turn to anyone else in the future when next you need lumber for a new addition to your home? I'd feel guilty going to a competitor when Pine Hill Lumber did such an imaginative and thought-provoking job helping us all to appreciate our founding and our heritage."

The kinds of public relations events that can be readily designed or implemented by small businesses include:

• Anniversaries and other chronological or seasonal commemorations (such as one firm's annual "Covered Wagon Day," to celebrate the arrival of the first settlers at the site)

• Annual sales and discount programs tied in with some fitting event (a local inn's complimentary "Deep South Oyster Roast" each New Year's Day to promote the date on which the inn served its first meal — native Port Royal Sound oysters — in 1876)

• The recognition of a regional holiday to associate the business with the historic event (Samuel J.G. Dewey Design Award, to commemorate the birth of the town's most prestigious Georgian architect who designed many of the town's buildings, including the plant in which the sponsor's manufacturing business has been located for almost a quarter of a century)

• Attendance at a biennial trade show and sponsorship of a prize for the most-visited booth (the prize in one instance being a commercial water filter by a local distributor who also supplies the water for the show itself)

• **Open houses,** in which you invite the public to see your shop or outlet (a plant nursery holds four seasonal open-house exhibits, with free one-hour seminars, to introduce potential customers to the joys of growing herbs, garden vegetables, bonsai dwarf trees, and the like)

• **Plant tours** to announce new facilities or equipment (one printing house holds an occasional "Print Jamboree," during which visitors are given free reign designing stationery and assisting with the production of such small items as calling cards, envelope labels, or self-adhesive stickers, compliments of the house)

• Public speaking assignments at nearby institutions (a pest-control firm scheduled a program of sending its specialists to speak about wildlife in, and outside of, private residences, restaurants, and various other commercial establishments)

• Sponsorship of scholarships or youth opportunities (such a program greatly enhanced the standing of an educational book wholesaler who awarded encyclopedias to top high-school students, as well as modest book allowances to first-year students accepted in any of the state's colleges).

While small businesses new to a neighborhood can benefit from P.R. programs like these, they are much more effective for a company that has become established over several years and has built a name for itself in its field and in ongoing community affairs and civic programs. The key word here is consistency. Once you decide which kind of activity is best suited, and the most valuable, to your public relations program, stick with it. A company image is not built overnight. It may, in fact, take two or three years to see any substantial progress. So if you start on one tack and then try another, and dabble in a third, you may never realize the kind of favorable recognition you want.

How to Select a Public Relations Agency

Public relations used to be quite simple. But today it has become so sophisticated that you may want to turn to the outside and hire a professional consultant, if not an active practitioner. According to Charles S. Phillips, who has had more than thirty years as a public relations generalist, "The public relations practitioner is taking on a new personality. Public

---

NEGOTIATING A WORKING CONTRACT

Whenever a business, even a small one, signs up with a public relations agency, a legal contract is vital to your working arrangements and objectives. Contracts range from very brief, informal ones to highly complex documents of many pages. Ask to see some sample contracts from any agency with which you intend to do business. Such a contract should define all or most of the following elements:

- *Services*. The types of activities and functions that will be provided
- *Compensation.* The basic fee, special fees, expenses, and hourly and per diem additions when approved
- *Billing procedures*. When and how the agency bills its clients, and periods when payments are due
- *Ownership*. Facts concerning the ownership of symbols, slogans, texts, pictures, or other materials created and supplied by the agency
- *Termination*. Dates on which the contract becomes effective and terminates, as well as an agreement regarding premature termination and release
- *Indemnification*. The joint and separate responsibilities of agency and client in the matter of accuracy, liabilities, claims, and the like
- *Purchasing*. Authority for the purchase of materials related to public relations, publicity, and other agreed-upon functions
- *Conflict of interest*. Agreement regarding the agency's right to represent other clients that might be wholly or partially competitive with the client.

---

relations people are no longer only writers and editors. They are business people . . . just as apt to be financial analysts or lawyers as they are journalists — people trained not only to *react* to news, but to *make* news by implementing programmed strategies . . . . They are being asked to wear many hats: those of versatile writer, press relations advisor, economic strategist, industrial psychologist, union relations counselor, employee motivator, government relations expert, and many more."

Of course, not all these functions may apply to your business. Mr. Phillips speaks from a high-level corporate standpoint. But there may be times when you feel the need for professional help in this area.

If your organization is large enough and prosperous enough to become a client of an established public relations agency, you need to do some homework to determine which one is most suited to your needs. It may be a branch office of a large P.R. firm, like Hill & Knowlton, Burson-Marsteller, or The Dilenschneider Group. Or it may be a local, one-office agency with relatively small accounts. In either case, you have to appoint a reliable, preferably experienced, manager in your own firm to act as P.R. liaison. According to Charles S. Phillips, "A beneficial agency–client relationship requires knowledge of the procedures involved in agency selection, a comprehension of budgets and contracts, and most important, how to use a public relations consultancy for maximum benefit."

There are more than 1,500 public relations firms in the United States. So the problem is not how to find one, but how to find one that will give you the most for your dollar. In recent years, there has been an increase in the number of small, specialized agencies. If your business is a special-interest type, appealing to a narrow market, you might want to consider whether this calls for an agency that specializes in reaching that market. These small shops focus on such areas as medicine and health, politics and government, travel, sports and recreation, retailing, environmental issues, foods and beverages, and transportation — to name just a few.

Agencies sometimes specialize also, in whole or in part, in demographic subject areas, supporting organizations that cater to groups according to ethnic, racial, sex, age, or religious backgrounds.

Evaluating a Public Relations Agency

When you have narrowed your choice to two or three agencies that seem the most compatible with your goals, ask yourself the following questions, as recommended by the Public Relations Society of America (PRSA):

• What is your impression of the agency, and specifically, its creative expertise?

• Do the people you have met understand your needs and objectives?

• Does the internal structure of the agency provide the right kind of support for your account?

• Have you been shown anything to document the agency's experience and success in your field, or in related fields?

• What are the agency's major strengths, especially in those areas where you think your own public relations and communications efforts are weak?

• Have you been given an estimate of costs to do the job, and, if so, are they reasonable?

• Would your account be important to this agency and not be put on the back burner?

• What media contacts does this agency have that are the most important to you?

• Are you at liberty to call some of the agency's clients to get their opinions?

• Would you and your associates feel comfortable and assured when working with this public relations firm?

CHAPTER TWELVE

Advertising in a Changing Climate

KEY TERMS FOR THIS CHAPTER

account executives   copywriters   marketing
audience   direct mail   medium (pl., media)
commercial   graphics   point-of-purchase displays
continuity   logo   sample

Many small-business owners and managers make the mistake of thinking of advertising principally as a means of announcing a new product or service. It is true that advertising to prospective customers can play a substantial role in determining the success or failure of a new venture. But the true test of advertising comes when it is time to keep the ball rolling and undertake the routine, if not dull, assignment of steadily building repeat business and a favorable reputation.

Advertising for Long-term Growth: A Case History

Several years ago, the concept of screen printing was little know to business managers. This

is a process that makes it possible for commercial establishments to print very small runs — such as for leaflets, posters, labels, and catalogs — at low cost. In addition to low cost, the screen printing has other advantages, for example, it permits the use of color, the ability to make text revisions at the last minute, and the flexibility to add personal messages.

Screen Ventures, a small company in California, typifies the way a number of firms in this field grew from shoestring operations into substantial organizations as a result of effective advertising programs. What they did, in effect was use the ad media to tell potential customers about business benefits they had not been aware of before. They used some obvious come-on ad techniques, describing the process as dramatic, versatile, vibrant, and creative. But they also backed up the colorful language with copy pointing out how users of screen printing would benefit from flexibility, low cost, full color, and image quality.

The advertisements heightened the credibility of the campaign by injecting appropriate notes of humor — a valuable commodity in the communications field. As one ad headlined, "The Only Thing that Can't Be Screen Printed is Money."

While no one can claim that advertising was the sole catalyst that spurred the company's upward momentum, it is fair to claim that advertising helped to pave the way.

Why Continue to Advertise?

The American Association of Advertising Agencies (known popularly as "The Four A's") lists four reasons for **continuity** in advertising:

1. It requires a considerable length of time for an advertising campaign to register with the public initially.

2. If a campaign is stopped, this same process has to be repeated at a later date when the advertiser again wants to generate public awareness.

3. Stop-and-go advertising, though it may seem to be cheaper (like turning your house lights on and off to save electricity), actually costs more because it requires more ads to achieve the same objectives.

4. A steady, low-budget advertising program is generally more effective than a series of high-cost blockbuster campaigns.

Advertising is multidimensional, playing three roles which, when carried out through a consistent advertising campaign, will reap ongoing benefits for you. These three roles of advertising are:

1. *A form of communication*, which permits the advertiser to reach targeted audiences through newspapers, magazines, television, radio, direct mail, billboards, and other media at a reasonable cost.

2. *A component of an economic system*, which supports a free market system in which consumers are likely to purchase products and services they see advertised or mentioned in articles, over the air, and through other editorial vehicles.

3. *A means of financing the mass media*. This is vital to the promotion and sale of goods and services because few media, such as magazines and broadcasting stations and newspapers, could exist without advertising support. The bonus for advertisers is that they frequently get free publicity through these media. It is economically sound and mutually beneficial for local businesses to support their community publications, broadcasting, and other media through advertising, within realistic and continuing budgets.

Advertising and Marketing — Their Relationship

Managers who have had little experience in this field find it difficult to distinguish advertising from **marketing**. Professor Don E. Schultz, a specialist in communications, explains the relationship this way: "Marketing is the master or king; advertising is one of many servants attending marketing. If a company really understands how to market its products, goods, and services, advertising is skillfully integrated as part of a whole plan, usually designed by the marketing manager."

Much of the relationship depends upon timing; the advertising should appear at the most propitious times during the marketing program. It is also essential that the themes used in the advertising tie in with the marketing goals. If, for example, you are marketing products that your salespeople claim are environmentally compatible, the focus of the advertising should be similar. If you are marketing a line of products that has a price advantage over those of

---

ADVERTISING INFORMATION RESOURCES

You can locate information about advertising and related subjects, when conducting your own research, in the following publications and sources:

- Library card catalogues
- Cumulative Book Index
- Reader's Guide to Periodical Literature
- Books in Print
- Business Periodical Index
- Business and financial periodicals, such as *The Wall Street Journal*, *Barron's*, *Forbes*, and *Inc*.
- Moody's Industrial Manual
- Standard and Poor's publications
- Corporate annual reports
- Encyclopedia of Business Information Sources
- U.S. Census publications
- Statistical Abstract of the United States
- County and city data books
- State statistical abstracts
- *Sales Management Magazine*'s annual issue, *Survey of Buying Power*
- Standard Rate and Data Service
- Simmons Market Research Bureau

---

your competitors, the advertising should concentrate on pricing. A third essential is the marketing region itself. Your advertising should use media that reaches this region completely and with a minimum of excess circulation.

Appropriate Media for Small Businesses

There are several communications vehicles commonly used by small businesses for advertising purposes. The importance of each depends upon the nature of the business and the products and services being promoted. Here are some of the media in which small businesses frequently advertise:

- *Newspapers.* Daily, weekly, and special-issue newspapers are consulted by readers in any given community for local information, including that supplied by advertisers. These papers are especially effective for announcements that combine commercial news with a picture or checklist that the reader can tear out, such as a holiday sale with itemized products and prices.

- *Radio.* This medium offers instantaneous reception and a personalized presentation at low cost.
- *Television.* While more expensive than radio, television is ideal for displaying products in an appealing manner. In some regions, cable TV offers better rates, making it more affordable for advertisers who want to repeat their message frequently.
- *Magazines.* These can be general, regional, specialized, or trade publications. Although more expensive than newspapers, they have a much longer life, as well as the capability of presenting clear visual details and high-quality pictorial effects.
- *Point-of-purchase displays.* Posters and cardboard cut-outs located with the merchandise being promoted are known as **point-of-purchase displays.** Although they can clinch sales, they rely on other advertising to bring prospective buyers to the store.
- *The Yellow Pages.* This is a well-documented source of business for many types of small businesses, and flexible enough to fit almost any budget.
- *Outdoor advertising.* This includes posters and billboards. Because of increasing opposition to outdoor signs, this medium should be used with discretion by small businesses and should be as tasteful as possible.
- *Direct mail.* Vehicles as letters, catalogs, leaflets, envelope stickers, postal imprints, contests, newsletters, coupons, timetables, programs, reprints, invitations, printed novelties, samples — in other words, just about anything that can be mailed at reasonable cost — are used in **direct-mail** marketing.

Which Medium Is for You?

How do you decide which individual **medium** or combination of media are best for your business? The bottom line is usually cost: first, the amount you pay to prepare the advertising and, second, the cost of reaching a specified number of readers or viewers through a selected medium. However, you also have to evaluate the impact the medium has — the force that motivates people to buy your products or use your services. You might find, for example, that it will cost you twice as much to reach 10,000 prospective buyers on TV as it would to send your message to the same number of people in a radio **commercial.** But if you are promoting a product that has great visual appeal and cannot be described easily in words alone, TV might be more cost-effective because of the number of actual purchasers delivered to you by the medium.

Another basic factor is timing. Do you want to reach your audience in the morning when people peruse the paper over breakfast? You might, if you have something to sell that will improve the quality of their coffee and motivate them to add your product to their daily shopping list. Or are you more interested in having your message in a magazine where people can read and think about it over a period of time? You might, if you are offering a home-decorating service or distinctive furniture pieces that require some consideration before a purchase decision is reached.

Think, too, of your **audience.** Why pay to reach a general audience of 100,000 people in a regional magazine when you are selling rods and reels and are really interested in the readers of a sports fishing newsletter that has a subscription list of only 12,000 — all avid fishermen who live nearby?

The Importance of Graphics

When you started in business, you probably created some kind of **logo** or trademark, which you have continued to use, perhaps improved upon or refined. It is important to maintain this form of **graphics** as an identifying part of your image. You should also have an identifying color or combination of colors for application with this logo or trademark.

Most businesses also find that it is advantageous to select and stick with a typeface that is distinctive and reflects the nature of their organization. An antiques shop, for example, might use a typeface that has a Victorian style; an electronics distributor a face that resembles a computer printout; and a fitness and health studio a face that is strong, bold, and modern.

Stick to your graphic image wherever your name or identification occurs, not only in ads, but on your building signs, letterheads, vehicles, equipment, work clothes, labels, order forms, samples and other giveaway items, business cards, and the like.

Audience Identification

Since you have been in business for some time, you have identified the audiences to which you address your advertising, correspondence, and other communications. Or have you? In the process of growth, you may be overlooking new audiences and extensions of existing audiences.

Finding New Audiences: Four Case Histories

Here are some typical cases of audiences that were overlooked by small businesses during periods of transition or growth:

• The producer and direct-mail vendor of shop and automotive tools always sent catalogs and promotional literature to men. He began to market a line of garden tools and, for many

months, sent these promotional materials also only to men — until his wife reminded him that women were just as interested in garden equipment.

• The owner of a shop that sold handbags, toilet kits, and other leather goods exclusively for ladies, tailored all her ads and promotions to women. As the business grew, she contracted with a local advertising agency and was surprised when the copywriter created some print ads aimed at men. As he explained to her, she was ignoring a substantial group of purchasers: men who bought leather goods as presents for wives, mothers, and daughters. As the business grew, she added merchandise of interest to both sexes, such as luggage, briefcases, and wallets.

• A firm that assembled and sold gymnasium and fitness products zeroed in exclusively on young adults as its audience for the sale of body-building equipment. It ascribes its later growth to the publication of a survey indicating that 26% of certain types of exercise equipment was being purchased by people over the age of 55. The firm's ad manager tailored some test ads for this market, describing his company as a "specialist in health-enhancing equipment for seniors." Sales jumped about 20% following the initiation of this ad campaign.

• An interior decorator with three regional outlets built a large and growing business by merchandising the firm's services only to offices, motels, and other such commercial establishments. She looked down at residential sales, which she considered too small and too time-consuming to be profitable. Then she realized that one of her outlets, which was near a high-priced retirement community, had by chance been called in to decorate several very expensive homes for absentee owners who were going to use them only five or six months each year. After doing some homework, she discovered that there was a large, untapped market

of business. It was profitable be-
...uyers did not want to become
personally involved and were willing to pay a
high price for a reliable, well-known professional to step in and deliver an entire decorating package. After running an ad program to
reach this kind of audience, sales (and profits)
began increasing steadily.

Professional **copywriters**, media specialists,
and **account executives** are trained to devote
a great part of their time to analyzing the
audiences they are most interested in reaching.
Before they ever sit down at the typewriter,
experienced copywriters will conduct research,
ask innumerable questions, and zero in on the
people to whom they are addressing their messages. Often, this process takes much longer
than the writing itself. If they find they do not
know all the answers and the ad budget will
permit, they sometimes recommend that a
study or survey be made to isolate the segments of the audience.

Selecting Your Audience

You should also devote time to determining
your most promising audience(s). There are
four categories by which an audience can be
classified:

1. *Demographic*, differentiating people by
age, sex, income, occupation, education, ethnic
background, faith, health, and marital status.

2. *Sociological*, focusing on their situation in
regard to social class, reference group, lifestyle,
status, and general role in the community.

3. *Geographical*, identifying location, nature and size of the community, existence of
strong local customs, climate, and seasonal
differentials.

4. *Psychological*, defining attitudes, beliefs,
values, motives, goals, predispositions, personality traits, and morals.

Consumer Surveys

If you have a limited budget for advertising,
but feel that a survey is necessary to determine
who you should be trying to reach, you might
undertake the job yourself or assign it to someone you can rely on to understand your objectives. When conducting or directing a limited
consumer research study, you should cover
these ten bases:

1. Establish a timetable and deadline, so
everyone involved knows exactly what you
want and when.

2. Specify exactly what it is you want to
learn.

3. Figure out approximately how many
people you have to reach to gather a meaningful **sample**, that is, a selection of people
large and varied enough so that this small
compilation provides a characteristic picture
of the whole.

4. Apportion your sample so you reach a
cross-section of the people who are significant
to your business.

5. Decide whether the most practical
method of collecting information is through
face-to-face interviews, phone calls, by mail, or
a combination of these methods.

6. Ask your Chamber of Commerce and/or
public library for related studies and surveys
that might supplement your information or perhaps help you to organize your own study.

7. Prepare a questionnaire that covers all
the subject areas you have in mind, but is not
too long or complex.

8. Keep close tabs on the project from day to
day to make sure you and your assistants are on
target. If there are any problems, seek solutions
and make revisions in the format or operations.

9. Tabulate the data, both in progress and
in final compilation.

10. Prepare a report, evaluating how best
you can use it to achieve your objective.

ADVERTISING FUNCTIONS PERTINENT TO SMALL BUSINESSES

Here is a list of activities your organization might be involved with when you have an active advertising campaign or program.

- Handling basic phases of preparing print ads and commercials
- Undertaking research and fact-finding
- Creating visual sales materials
- Preparing slides for use by salespeople
- Designing and producing dealer displays
- Preparing leaflets and catalogs
- Preparing and sending out mailings
- Editing an informational newsletter
- Arranging for samples and giveaways
- Planning prizes and awards
- Sponsoring brief seminars or orientation meetings
- Designing, building, and staffing trade show booths
- Preparing speeches and promotional releases.

Creating the Ad

Once you know your intended audience, you are in a good position to schedule the writing of copy for print ads and literature and scripts for broadcast commercials or other audio-visual presentations. At this point, you have to make some decisions, asking yourself these questions, among others:

- What is our primary audience?
- What are our secondary audiences?
- What kinds of ads should we prepare?
- What primary media shall we use?
- What secondary media, if any, should we consider?
- What is our budget for the present? In the long-term?
- What benchmarks can we use to measure the validity of our program and the success or failure of our campaign?
- Do we have any way of conceptualizing and executing our campaign based on successes or failures of past promotions and ad campaigns?

With these points clear, the actual writing and preparation of layouts (if pertinent) can begin. Whoever undertakes these creative efforts will emphasize the major benefits your product(s) or service(s) have to offer; will speak most directly to the target audience(s) you have

WHAT DO YOU NEED TO KNOW ABOUT MEDIA?

This worksheet is designed to help you evaluate major advertising vehicles that are important to consider, if not for the present, then for the short-term and long-range future.

	Potential	Advantages/Disadvantages
PRINT MEDIA		
Regional magazines		
Local magazines		
Daily newspapers		
Weekly newspapers		
Tabloid-style papers		
Special editions		
Supplements		
Shoppers		
Other		
BROADCASTING		
Radio		
Television		
Cassettes		
Videotapes		
POINT-OF-PURCHASE AND GRAPHICS		
Billboards and signs		
Point-of-purchase Displays		
Posters		
Giveaways		
Prizes		
Booths		
MAIL ORDER AND PHONE MARKETING		
Sales letters		
Mail campaigns		
Catalogs		
Telephone Solicitation		
Yellow Pages		
Other media to consider:		

already clarified; and will suggest ways to expedite the planned campaign most effectively.

Growth Through Advertising

Many corporations have grown and prospered, not only because they had something to offer the public, but because they were adept at getting their messages across clearly and forcefully. The following are just a few examples of almost 100 such organizations listed in *The Vital Corporation,* a book by Garry Jacobs and Robert MacFarlane.

• The Old New York Brewery Company built its business by advertising that it produced a drink brewed the old-fashioned way, for people who were tired of the low-quality, mass-produced products touted by the big companies.

• Mesa Airlines, a small carrier spawned in New Mexico when the commercial airline industry was deregulated, competed with the majors by advertising and promoting short-span commuter services in markets where there was a stable demand.

• Linear Technology specialized in computer chips and expanded rapidly because it promoted a reputation for quality of product, quality of service, reliability, and punctuality.

• Precision Grinding and Manufacturing, a $10 million company with 125 employees jumped from heavy losses to substantial profits in one year by improving its performance and then letting potential customers know about its reliability and on-time delivery.

Advertising and promotion cannot be effective when a company's products, services, or operations leave something to be desired. But if you really have superior products or services and fail to advertise them actively and continuously, you may be in just as much a bind as if you had very little to offer. Advertising is a critical segment of an overall marketing strategy to help keep your business growing.

Counseling for Growth

The image of an entrepreneur who has launched a business, stimulated its growth, profited, and in all other ways earned the mark of success is that of a self-made person, a leader who can continue to guide the business to even greater heights. "Entrepreneurs are likely to exude confidence and show real determination to do it themselves and call the signals," says Curt Ivey, a man who has built several successful small businesses that have continued to expand. "However," he adds, "many of them operate on one plateau and never climb to the summits they could reach if they would only admit that they are not superhuman and would occasionally seek out professional consultants who can provide further guidance, as well as objectivity."

No matter how strong your confidence in yourself may be, you should bear in mind that today's economic complexities are such that very few owners of small businesses can ignore the help of **specialists** to improve their profits

and escalate their growth. Few entrepreneurs would hesitate to go to an investment broker to purchase stocks, to a banker to negotiate a loan, or to an engineer to design foundations for a plant. Yet many of these same people feel it is a sign of managerial weakness to call in **consultants** on such matters as marketing, the recruitment of personnel, negotiating joint ventures, or redesigning office and commercial layouts.

Small businesses most frequently seek outside professionals in the area of legal services and advice. Many businesses cannot function properly without an outside attorney, at least on a part-time basis. Yet there are literally dozens upon dozens of other types of consultants you can turn to, regardless of how specialized or narrow your business may be. *The Directory of Management Consultants*, published by Consultant News, lists almost 1,000 consulting firms in more than 120 subject areas, ranging from automation and diversification to quality control, attitude studies, pricing policies, postal services, union avoidance, tariffs, licensing, security, appraising, behavior, dealer support, and commodities.

For a more comprehensive overview of consulting fields, you have to turn to other directories, such as *Consultants & Consulting Organizations*, published by Gale Research.

Do You Need Consultation?

Take a piece of paper and jot down in a column the essential elements and factors of your business, such as sales, marketing, advertising, public relations, accounting, taxes, insurance, training, safety, computers and electronic data processing, recruiting, employee benefits, communications, transportation, financing, investments, community relations, government regulations, and the like.

Next to each of these entries, in a separate column, jot down as honestly as you can your own familiarity, skill, and experience in each of these areas. Rate them Excellent, Moderate, or Minimal, as the case may be.

Next, use a third column to indicate whether you have one or more experts in your company who rate an Excellent mark in any of these areas.

Now you will have a pretty good idea of the functions that need outside assistance in order to have your business operating on all cylinders. Make another list to indicate the weak spots that could be strengthened, placing the entries in order of importance or urgency. Having established your priorities, you are now in a position to investigate sources of professional assistance and estimate the costs you would have to pay for consultation. Fortunately, consultants are generally needed only for one-shot projects, such as making a **feasibility study** for a new plant location, upgrading the efficiency of manufacturing procedures, conserving water or basic materials used in operations, solving environmental and pollution problems, or providing **demographic data** about a new community to which you intend to extend your business.

Other consulting services are those that are periodic, such as annual assistance to interpret new tax laws, or those that are long-range, such

---

SOURCES OF INFORMATION

Among the many sources of information about consulting assistance are the following:

General	*Professional*	*Governmental*
Chambers of Commerce	Lawyers	Small Business
Business friends	Accountants	Administration
Local service clubs	Advertising executives	Department of Commerce
Fraternal organizations	Bankers	Municipal and state agencies
Your own customers or	Trade associations	Educational institutions
clients	Suppliers	Public libraries
General newspapers		
Friendly competitors		

LOCATING THE RIGHT CONSULTANT

1. Decide whether you want a consultant who is a **generalist,** providing expertise in most of the fields that are basic to small business, or a specialist, whose capabilities are narrower but more in depth in a given area.

2. Consider whether you want to deal with a large firm, which may assure a greater range of coverage, or a small firm that may be more limited but provide personal service.

3. Consult a directory and list the firms that are within reach and that seem to cover the subject areas of concern.

4. Send for literature that describes their services, and ask about rates and contracts.

5. Obtain objective outside information about the candidates you have selected.

6. Narrow the field to two or three and set up interviews at whatever location is mutually convenient. Do not hesitate to bring along a third party, such as your attorney or advertising account executive, if you feel more comfortable.

7. Ask them for a proposal with the specifics of what they can do to help you. This should be in the form of a written presentation.

8. If all else is in order, request a draft of a contract, or other document, that would cover all necessary commitments by both parties.

9. Find out what individuals would be servicing your account and request their resumes and a chance to meet them.

---

as the development and implementation of a continuing advertising program.

Low-cost Consulting

Sometimes you can save money by sharing consulting expenses with another company when you have mutual problems in certain areas, such as installing filter systems when the local water supply contains ingredients harmful to certain processing functions. Don't overlook free consultation and assistance offered by some utilities and other common service organizations. Energy companies, for example, will usually conduct extensive studies of oil, gas, and electric rates and recommend ways you can conserve energy — and costs — by revising your current system. Telephone companies commonly review rates and services of their customers, large and small, to advise them about ways to cut costs and improve service.

Before spending money for a consultant, ask yourself whether you are a customer of any businesses whose owners or managers could be talked into an assist in their area of expertise without sending you a bill. The owner of a large retail store selling women's apparel was presented with plans for improving displays and racks by a dress wholesaler from whom she purchased merchandise regularly. An entrepreneur who was about to hire an expert to redesign and enlarge the craft shop where he and five assistants made leather goods, turned instead to the leather manufacturer's association of which he was a member; he obtained the services of a highly experienced specialist who spent three days on the assignment at no cost except his daily travel expenses and lunches. The owners of an automotive repair service get all the consultation they need from the suppliers of their products and tools. And, of course, anyone who has a **franchise** can expect built-in assistance from the franchise organization without having to go elsewhere.

Associations are often one of the prime sources of counsel and help, though you have to read the small print in every case. The American Small Business Association (ASBA) and National Small Business United (NSBU) promote themselves as organizations that assist entrepreneurs with day-to-day business problems, for example. There is a slight catch here in that some associations also want to sell insurance policies as well as memberships. You have to decide — no matter where you turn — whether the advice you get is really free or whether you are paying for it in a hidden manner. In some cases, it is worth it.

Don't overlook the Service Corps of Retired Executives (SCORE), which can be found in most telephone directories and business listings. SCORE is made up of volunteers, who provide their services at no cost to small businesses and entrepreneurs in their community. Since the members have all been experienced business persons before retiring, they have a wealth of general advice and can also steer you to members who are specialists in their fields.

Worksheets: Are You Prepared to Grow Your Business?

PERSONAL SKILLS SURVEY

After achieving success, many small-business owners find that their enterprise levels off and they cannot maintain the same pace. It is never too early to take stock of your personal attributes and capabilities and relate them to what is needed to continue the pattern of growth.

The essentials to consider are:

EDUCATIONAL ELEMENTS

Reading habits that contribute to business and professional knowledge _____

_____

Meetings and conferences that broaden my views or provide data of value _____

_____

Available courses that could improve my present capabilities _____

_____

Subject areas in which I am strong _____

_____

Subject areas in which I am weak _____

_____

People inside the company who could help to orient me on certain topics _____

_____

People (contacts) outside the company to whom I could turn for orientation, either free or at cost _____

LEADERSHIP CHARACTERISTICS

Ability to communicate _____

_____

First-hand knowledge of jobs and assignments of people who work for me _____

_____

Ability to judge people _____

_____

Facility at establishing priorities

Grasp of situations and circumstances, both commonplace and unusual

Rapport with people, both inside and outside the company

Effectiveness at motivating people to work on behalf of our objectives

Decision-making qualities

Willingness to seize the initiative

Sympathy for others, especially in sensitive situations

Sound judgment

Powers of persuasion

Self-control in trying situations

Readiness to listen to others, at all levels

Genuine interest in people and what motivates them

IMAGINATION AND CREATIVITY

Conviction that creative efforts are fun, as well as productive

Powers of imagination

Ability to conceptualize in terms understandable to other people

Sense of humor

Rating creativity high when reviewing candidates for jobs or assignments

Originality

Resourcefulness

Power to concentrate _____

Fascination with approaches and procedures that are different _____

Innovative skills _____

Ability to visualize and make rough, if not finished, sketches of subjects _____

Preference for people who are not afraid to express ideas, even though controversial _____

NO-NONSENSE QUIZ: OVERALL QUALIFICATIONS

It is relatively easy for most entrepreneurs to ask themselves whether they have the technical skill to operate a manufacturing business, the grasp of monetary matters to deal with financial challenges, or the experience and training to develop effective marketing plans.

But ask yourself, in all honesty, whether you qualify in areas that are more personal and intangible. Like these, for example:

How do I really feel about managing people, as well as business operations? _____

Do I assume responsibility willingly? _____

Can I make decisions without agonizing over the pros and cons? _____

Am I really glad to see my business grow, or would I prefer to cut back a little? _____

When I propose ideas that may be somewhat off the usual course, do people trust my instincts? _____

Am I likely to be stubborn when I have an idea that my colleagues try to shoot down? ___
_____

Do I hold grudges? _____
_____

Can I forgive my employees and others who make serious, but honest, mistakes? _____
_____

Am I able to work long hours sometimes, as needed, without becoming a workaholic? ___
_____

Am I able to delegate responsibilities well, particularly as the business grows? _____
_____

Do I approach projects with vigor and enthusiasm, even if I may be feeling temporarily under the weather? _____
_____
_____

Bibliography

Selected reference sources for information on growing your small business successfully:

Books

Bangs, David H., Jr., and White, Steve. *The Business Planning Guide*. Dover, NJ: Upstart Publishing Company, 1986.

Bates, James. *The Management of Small Business*. London: Philip Allan, 1989.

Berry, Don. *Small Business Borrowers Guide*. New York: Law Forum, 1988.

Blumenthal, Lasser. *Successful Business Writing*. New York: Putnam, 1985.

Burstiner, Irving. *Run Your Own Store: Proven Strategies for Profit in Every Type of Retail Business*. 2nd ed. New York: Prentice-Hall, 1989.

Cohn, Theodore, and Lindberg, Roy. *Survival and Growth for Small Business*. New York: Amacom, 1980.

Consultants News. *Directory of Managements Consultants*. Fitzwilliam, New Hampshire: Consultants News, annual.

Cross, Wilbur. *Action Letters for Small Business Owners*. New York: Wiley, 1991.

Cullinan, Mary. *Business Communication: Principles and Processes*. New York: Holt, Rinehart & Winston, 1989.

Day, William H. *Maximizing Small Business Profits with Precision Management*. Englewood Cliffs, NJ: Prentice-Hall, 1979.

Dreyfack, Ray. *Sure Fail: The Art of Mismanagement*. New York: Morrow, 1976.

Elster, Robert J., ed. *Small Business Sourcebook*. Detroit, MI: Gale, 1989.

Frantz, Forest H. *Successful Small Business Management*. Englewood Cliffs, NJ: Prentice-Hall, 1978.

Friedman, Paul B. *Making It: How to Succeed in Your Own Small Business*. Helena, MT: Falcon, 1984.

Gale Research Company. *Encyclopedia of Associations*. Detroit, MI: Gale, annual.

Gallagher, Richard R. *Your Small Business Made Simple*. New York: Doubleday, 1989.

Garofalo, Gene. *Sales Managers Desk Book*. Englewood Cliffs, NJ: Prentice-Hall, 1989.

Goldstein, *Small Business Legal Problem Solver*. New York: Van Nostrand Reinhold, 1984.

Goldstick, Gary. *Business Rx: How to Get in the Black and Stay There*. New York: Wiley, 1988.

Hawken, Paul. *Grow Your Own Business*. New York: Simon & Schuster, 1987.

Hull, Christopher. *Helping Small Firms Grow*. New York: Routledge, Chapman & Hall, 1988.

Jacobs, Garry, and MacFarlane, Robert. *The Vital Corporation*. Englewood Cliffs, NJ: Prentice-Hall, 1990.

Justis, Robert T. *Managing Your Small Business*. Englewood Cliffs, NJ: Prentice-Hall, 1981.

Kline, John B. *Managing the Small Business*. Homewood, IL: Irwin, 1982.

Lawrence, Peter, ed. *Small Business Breakthrough*. Cambridge, MA: Blackwell, 1985.

MacFarlane, W. *Principles of Small Business Management*. New York: McGraw-Hill, 1977.

McCormack, Mark H. *What They Don't Teach You at the Harvard Business School*. New York: Bantam, 1984.

Megginson, Leon C. *Successful Small Business Management*. Homewood, IL: Irwin, 1988.

Metcalf, et. al. *How to Make Money in Your Own Small Business*. Englewood Cliffs, NJ: Prentice-Hall, 1981.

————. *The Barriers to Growth in Small Firms*. New York: Routledge, Chapman & Hall, 1989.

Moreau, James F. *Effective Small Business Management*. Boston: Houghton Mifflin, 1980.

Park, William R., and Chapin-Park, Sue. *How to Succeed in Your Own Business*. New York: Wiley, 1978.

Phillips, Charles. *Secrets of Successful Public Relations*. Englewood Cliffs, NJ, 1985.

Resnic, Paul. *The Small Business Bible: The Make-or-Break Factors for Survival and Success*. New York: Wiley, 1988.

Rogoff, Leonard. *Office Guide to Business Letters, Memos, and Reports*. New York: Arco, 1984.

Seglin, Jeffrey L. *The AMA Handbook of Business Letters*. New York: Amacom, 1989.

Silvester, James L. *How to Start, Finance, and Operate Your Own Business*. New York: Lyle Stuart, 1984.

Smith, Brian. *Raising Seed Money for Your Own Business*. New York: Greene, 1984.

Steinhoff, Daniel, and Burgess, John. *Small Business Management Fundamentals*. New York: McGraw-Hill, 1988.

Tate, Curtis E., Jr. *Successful Small Business Management*. Plano, TX: Business Publications, 1985.

Timmons, Jeffrey A. *New Venture Creation: A Guide to Small Business Development*. Homewood, IL: Irwin, 1985.

Wilson, Brian. *The Small Business Handbook*. New York: Blackwell, 1985.

Woy, Patricia A. *Small Businesses that Grow and Grow and Grow*. Crozet, VA: Betterway Publications, 1989.

Periodicals

The following periodicals are of special interest to the owners and managers of small businesses:

Advertising Age, 740 North Rush Street, Chicago, IL 60611
American Business, 1775 Broadway, New York, NY 10019
Business Week, 1221 Avenue of the Americas, New York, NY 10020
Changing Times, 1279 H Street, NW, Washington, DC 20006

Direct Marketing, 224 Seventh Street, Garden City, NY 11530

Entrepreneur, 2311 Pontius Avenue, Los Angeles, CA 90064

Home Business News, 12221 Beaver Pike, Kackson, OH 45640

Inc. Magazine, 38 Commercial Wharf, Boston, MA 02110

Income Opportunities, 380 Lexington Avenue, New York, NY 10017

Kiwanis Magazine, 3636 Woodview Trace, Indianapolis, IN 46268

Management World, 2360 Maryland Road, Willow Grove, PA 19090

Marketing News, 250 South Wacker Drive, Chicago, IL 60606

Money Magazine, 1271 Avenue of the Americas, New York, NY 10020

Nation's Business, 1615 H Street, NW, Washington, DC 20062

New Business, 948 Florida Avenue, Sarasota, FL 33577

New England Business, 33 Union Street, Boston, MA 02108

Opportunity Magazine, 6 North Michigan Avenue, Chicago, IL 60602

Personnel Journal, 245 Fischer Avenue, Costa Mesa, CA 92626

Potentials in Marketing, 50 South 9th Street, Minneapolis, MN 55402

Stores, 100 West 31st Street, New York, NY 10001

Success Magazine, 342 Madison Avenue, New York, NY 10173

Venture, 521 Fifth Avenue, New York, NY 10175

Resources

Some Key Professional Associations that Support Small Business

Active Corps of Executives
c/o Small Business Association
1441 L Street, NW
Washington, DC 20416

American Business Women's Association
P.O. Box 8728
9100 Ward Parkway
Kansas City, MO 64114

American Federation of Small Business
407 South Dearborn Street
Chicago, IL 60605

American Entrepreneurs Association
2392 Morse Avenue
Irvine, CA 92713

Association of Data Processing Service
  Organizations
1300 North 17th Street, Suite 300
Arlington, VA 22209

Center for Family Business
P.O. Box 24268
Cleveland, OH 44124

International Council for Small Business
3550 Lindell Boulevard
St. Louis, MO 63103

International Entrepreneurs Association
2311 Pontius Avenue
Los Angeles, CA 90064

National Business League
4324 George Avenue, NW
Washington, DC 20011

National Federation of Independent
  Business
150 West 20th Avenue
San Mateo, CA 94403

National Small Business Association
NSB Building
1604 K Street, NW
Washington, DC 20006

Service Corps of Retired Executives
c/o Small Business Administration
1441 L Street, NW
Washington, DC 20416

Small Business Legislative Council
1604 K Street, NW
Washington, DC 20006

United States Chamber of Commerce
1615 H Street, NW
Washington, DC 20062

Small Business Administration (SBA): Regional Offices

Region I
155 Federal Street
9th Floor
Boston, MA 02110
(617) 451-2030

Region II
26 Federal Plaza
Room 31-08
New York, NY 10278
(212) 264-7772

Region III
Allendale Square
Suite 201
475 Allendale Road
King of Prussia, PA 19406
(215) 962-3805

Region IV
1375 Peachtree Street, NE
5th Floor
Atlanta, GA 30367-8102
(404) 347-2797

Region V
300 S. Riverside Plaza
Suite 1975
Chicago, IL 60606-6611
(312) 353-0359

Region VI
8625 King George Dr.
Building C
Dallas, TX 75235-3391
(214) 767-7643

Region VII
911 Walnut Street
13th Floor
Kansas, MO 64106
(816) 426-2989

Region VIII
999 18th Street
Suite 701, N. Tower
Denver, CO 80202
(303) 294-7001

Region IX
71 Stevenson St.
San Francisco, CA 94105-2939
(415) 744-6402

Region X
2615 Fourth Avenue
Room 440
Seattle, WA 98121
(206) 442-5676

Glossary

account executive In an advertising agency, the person assigned to supervise a client's account.

account payable A liability to a creditor, usually for goods and services.

account receivable A claim against a debtor, usually for products delivered or services rendered.

acquisition In business terminology, usually a company or other substantial entity acquired.

advertising The action of attracting public attention and potential customers through various paid media.

assets The entries on an organization's balance sheet showing financial and tangible properties that are owned or that can be readily converted to ownership.

bar chart A business chart that uses vertical or horizontal bars proportionately to give a quick, visual impression of related or comparable data and statistics.

break-even point The point at which profits and losses are in balance.

brochure A printed publication, usually larger than a leaflet, that describes a company, products, services, or other related information, for distribution to readers interested in the organization and/or its products and services.

business climate The attitudes and outlooks, as well as economic conditions, that prevail in any given locale.

capital Any form of material wealth, such as money or property, used or accumulated by an individual or organization.

capitalization As traditionally used in finance, the sum of the par value of a company's stocks and bonds outstanding.

cash flow The movement of money into and out of a business.

certificate of incorporation A legal document certifying that an organization has been established as a corporation.

certified public accountant (CPA) An accountant who meets various prescribed requirements, including the passing of a uniform examination prepared by the American Institute of Certified Public Accountants.

circulation As applied to advertising, particularly magazines and newspapers, the number of copies of a publication sent to a standard list of readers, whether free or by subscription, and sold at newsstands and other retail outlets.

collaboration Working jointly with one or more individuals or organizations in a mutual venture.

collateral Security pledged against an obligation, such as stocks used to cover a loan.

common stock Ordinary capital shares of a corporation that have claim on the net assets of the organization after other obligations have been paid.

compatible A business system or operation that functions harmoniously with a complementary one.

compensation Money or other valuables given, or received, for service or contribution.

consultant A professional expert or specialist who advises clients and is paid a one-time fee or a continuing retainer.

copyright The exclusive right, granted by law to any individual or group, to sell or reproduce an original work, generally extending for the life of the author plus 50 years after his or her death, if the work was created in or after 1978.

corporation A body of persons legally granted the right to be a separate entity distinct from those of its members.

cost control A business system devised to supervise, monitor, and control certain costs, whether specific or general.

decentralization The distribution of administrative powers or functions among individuals or groups other than those in central headquarters.

demographics Data researched and computed statistically to present specific information about the makeup of population segments. Such information might categorize people by sex, age, education, background, and income.

depreciation Recognized decrease in value because of wear and tear, damage, or decline in price.

direct mail Mail addressed directly by an organization to prospective customers or clients during advertising, promotion, or merchandising campaigns.

distribution In commerce, the process of moving goods from the manufacturer to the consumer or point of sale.

diversification The act of extending a business into other fields, related or unrelated, in order to increase profits or otherwise improve the value of the organization.

electronic data processing Popularly referred to as EDP, a process whereby electronic computers are used to organize the compilation of information.

employee turnover The nature and degree to which employees are joined to or released from an organization.

entrepreneur A person who creates, organizes, and operates a business venture. (Derived from the French *entreprendre,* to undertake.)

equity The basic value of a business or property beyond any liabilities connected with it.

equity capital That portion of a business's capital that is furnished by stockholders.

excise An indirect tax levied on the production, sale, or consumption of certain commodities, such as tobacco or alcohol, within a country.

expenses, fixed Expenses that change very little or not at all during any specific period.

expenses, variable Expenses that commonly change from one period to the next and seldom remain fixed for any length of time.

facilities In business, a term used to designate structures or equipment on hand to facilitate an action or process.

forecasting In business or commercial operations, the action undertaken to determine what future events will be significant to an organization's status.

franchise Authorization granted by a manufacturer or other key business to a dealer, distributor, or independent operator to sell his products or services, generally in a retail outlet or facility.

fringe benefits Benefits or things of value given to employees other than their wages or salaries.

graphics Illustrations, charts, or other visualizations used in advertising and promotion, for commercial presentations, and for training.

gross income The overall income received by a company prior to deductions, such as expenses, taxes, and interest.

growth, controlled The monetary or physical growth of an organization that is controlled so it does not exceed certain limits during any given period of time or in any designated area.

growth, explosive Uncontrolled, and generally undesirable, expansion of a company or other organization.

guaranty loan A commercial loan that is guaranteed (or assumed) by a person or organization other than the one receiving the loan.

hardware In connection with computers, the physical equipment such as the keyboard and printer and monitor used in the process of compiling and storing information.

human resources The personnel used directly or indirectly to perform the necessary functions and operations, as contrasted to the physical and mechanical resources.

incorporation The act of establishing a business legally as a corporation.

inventory The total quantity of goods and materials held by a company or organization.

job description A formalized statement used by a company to define the nature, responsibilities, and duties of a specific job or assignment, and usually the remuneration promised.

joint venture A venture or enterprise in which two or more individuals or organizations agree to join forces for their mutual strength and benefit.

layout, architectural The floor plan, and associated elements for an office, plant, or other structure.

layout, art The arrangement of visual elements on a page for an advertisement or other print medium.

liability An obligation or debt for which an individual or an organization is responsible.

limited partnership A business partnership of two or more people, organized legally in such a way that individual responsibilities and liabilities regarding the business are limited and not necessarily shared equally.

logo, logotype A trademark or symbol to identify a company.

management The person or persons who manage a business or institution and who determine the nature of the operation, its objectives, and the personnel needed for the overall performance.

market Commercially, the size, location, and nature of the area in which a company can logically and realistically conduct its business.

marketing That function in a company that is directly concerned with the sale and distribution of products and materials or the activity of providing services to the public.

markup The amount added to the cost of materials or products, usually calculated to take into account the expense of overhead and the desired profit.

media In advertising and marketing, the plural of *medium* is commonly used to refer to all means of mass communication, such as newspapers, radio, TV, and magazines, that are used as vehicles for conveying information to consumers.

merchandising The promotion of goods and services, whether by advertising, publicity, sales programs, word of mouth, or combinations thereof, to help move goods from manufacturers to consumers.

net income Income retained by a company after the gross income has been cut by costs, taxes, fees, losses, and other deductions.

operations Those functions of a company that are designated by a combination of machines, manpower, equipment, and energy to accomplish specified objectives.

organizational chart A graphic chart, table, or diagram depicting the positions and relationships of people in an organization, or the layout of different departments.

orientation Introductory instructions covering a new situation or procedure.

owner's equity The basic value in a company, or share of its stock, assigned to the owner.

partnership A business contract entered into by two or more persons in which each agrees to share the expenses, labor, and responsibilities in a joint enterprise.

personnel The employees of an organization.

point of purchase The location at which the customers select goods they are going to buy in a retail establishment.

policy An overall plan or course of action in a business organization designed to guide managers and employees in making long-range actions and decisions for the common good.

presentation In advertising or business planning, a proposal made by one party to another in the form of verbal and/or graphic communications.

press release An announcement or account of circumstances or actions or other news in letter form, distributed by an organization to members of the press.

print media Newspapers, magazines, and other periodicals that are printed on paper and read by recipients, in contrast to other media, such as radio, that reach audiences over the air.

profit A gain or return, whether in cash or other valuables beneficial to the organization.

profit-and-loss (P&L) statement An account showing net and gross profit or loss over a given period of time.

promotion In marketing, an individual effort or a long-range campaign that is designed to help sell a company's products or services to prospective customers.

proposal A formal presentation of data designed to encourage the recipient or audience to view the creator's suggestions favorably.

prospect A person who is a likely purchaser of products or services, or seems favorably inclined to join an organization or agree to a point of view.

public relations The actions and methods employed by an individual or organization to promote public goodwill in regard to the person(s) engaged in the promotion.

publicity The act of distributing information or sponsoring an activity to generate favorable public interest.

quality control Systems and procedures designed to maintain quality in manufacturing, production, or processing.

readership The total number of people who read a periodical, such as a newspaper or magazine; it is determined by multiplying the circulation by the average number of people who read the periodical in question.

real property Buildings, structures, land, and in many cases inherent natural resources.

retail The sales of products, goods, and related services directly to consumers in limited quantities.

risk management The administration of plans, methods, and arrangements to reduce loss through various methods, such as security systems, insurance, and personnel training.

S Corporation A company incorporated specifically as a small business, with a limited number of stockholders and liability, and with a lower tax burden than a regular corporation.

sales tax A tax levied as a percentage of the price of products and services dispensed most commonly by a retailer or wholesaler.

saturation point In marketing and merchandising, the point that has been reached in sales beyond which there can be no increase in the number of prospective purchasers of products or services.

self-employment A situation whereby individuals earn their incomes through their own business, rather than as employees of someone else.

self-employment tax A tax assessment for people classified as "self-employed," in their own business.

service business An enterprise engaged largely in providing services rather than goods, products, or materials.

short-term money Money borrowed for a brief period of time at a specified rate of interest. It is usually dissolved with one or, at most, two to three payments.

software Programs that are prepared specifically to activate computers to provide and/or store data as instructed.

sole proprietorship A small business that is wholly owned and controlled by one person.

specialization The act of engaging in business operations that are limited in nature or concentrated in a particular area.

specialty goods Merchandise for sale that is limited in scope, application, and usefulness, such as health foods, garden tools, sewing materials, or craft supplies.

state of the art Systems, products, or equipment that represent the latest in technological advancement.

stock option A fringe benefit granting employees the option to purchase stock in the company, usually at a reduced price or with a matching gift of stock by their employer.

supplier The individual or organization that supplies a business enterprise with products, equipment, and supplies, usually on a continuing basis.

table Statistically, an orderly display of data in the form of a chart, or similar graphics, to present facts and figures quickly and succinctly.

term money Money borrowed for a long period of time and repaid in installments. Interest may be fixed or variable. Collateral is usually required.

trademark A distinguishing symbol, legally registered for the exclusive use of the organization that intends to use it as a sign of recognition.

traffic pattern The arrangement of space in a commercial building or manufacturing plant that facilitates the flow of personnel, goods, or equipment in the course of operations or the conduct of business.

vendor A seller of goods and supplies to a business.

venture capital Funds made available for investment in an unproven enterprise; sometimes referred to as "risk capital."

warranty A stipulation, explicit or implied, in assurance of some particular in regard to a contract or business dealing that the quality of goods is what has been stated and that reparation will be made if this is not true.

wholesale The sale of goods in large quantities, most commonly to a retailer, but not infrequently to consumers direct.

withholding That portion of an employee's pay that is placed in reserve and not paid, in order to meet predetermined personal financial obligations, most commonly the payment of income taxes.

word processor A computer that is equipped with a keyboard similar to that of a typewriter, which is used specifically for writing and editing texts.

workers' compensation Payments that are required by law to be made to an employee who is injured in the course of performing his or her work.

INDEX